Paul Ripley's
Expert Driving

Paul Ripley's
Expert Driving

by

Paul Ripley

with

Peter Amey

RIGHT WAY
plus

𝕿𝖍𝖊 𝕯𝖆𝖎𝖑𝖞 𝕿𝖊𝖑𝖊𝖌𝖗𝖆𝖕𝖍

Typeset in 10½ pt Legacy Serif Book by Letterpart Ltd., Reigate, Surrey.

Printed and bound in Great Britain by Mackays of Chatham.

The *Right Way Plus* series is published by Elliot Right Way Books, Brighton Road, Lower Kingswood, Tadworth, Surrey, KT20 6TD, U.K. For information about our company and the other books we publish, visit our web site at www.right-way.co.uk

Contents

Dedication

We would like to thank Sir John Whitmore for all the help he has given us with the formulation of our thoughts on the mental development of drivers. John is a sports psychologist and former European Saloon Car Champion who has applied his experience to the problems of road driving and has led the way in showing how to put brainpower before horsepower.

About the Authors

Paul Ripley is recognised as Britain's premier driving expert and held in the highest esteem by the automotive and driver training industry.

He has been involved in teaching the art of driving for the past 25 years. He is highly qualified in this role having attained the following:

DOT ADI Highest grade 6,
DIA Dip DI DIA Diploma in Driving Instruction,
DIA Diamond Advanced Instructor,
Grade A Cardington Special Driving Test (DOT),
RoSPA Gold – Grade 1 Driver (since 1984),
High Performance Course – HPC Member,
Mercedes-Benz Intensive Safety Course – Melsheim,
IAM Test Certificate,
RoSPA Diploma in Advanced Instruction.

Academically he holds:

City and Guilds 730 Teaching Diploma,
DIA – 5 Module Diploma in Driving Instruction,
RoSPA Diploma Course Advanced Teaching Certificate,
Carmen's Company Royal Logistic Safety Award for 2001, for his consistent, professional and accurate Safety promotion, year on year and week by week.

He is also highly qualified in circuit driving having attended the following circuit/racing schools:

Winfield Racing School – Magnys Cours – 1984,
Silverstone Racing School – Advanced and Racing Student
1982 – 1984,
Jim Russell Racing Drivers' School – Snetterton and Donnington
Scholarship 1983,
Brands Hatch Racing School – Brands Hatch/Oulton Park
1981 – 1986,
Micky Pillete Racing School – Zolder, Belgium – 1983,
Team Touraco – Cadwell Park – 1986,
96 Club – Chief Instructor – 1989.

Paul has developed his circuit/racing skills by driving on most of the British and European circuits, as well as spending time on proving grounds at Millbrook, MIRA, LTC, Lotus, Elvington and Gaydon.

He is also an experienced motorcyclist and owns a Ducati 916 Senna 2 and a Ducati 900 superlight. He has attended the following motorcycle courses:

Keith Code Californian Bike School – Levels 1 & 2 – 1996,
Keith Code Californian Bike School – Levels 2 and advanced 3 – 1997,
Ron Haslam Honda Racing School – Donnington – 1997,
Nurburgring Experience – Germany 1998.

Paul Ripley's regular inputs on many TV driving programmes, including Channel 4's 'DRIVEN', have earned him the enviable title of 'The Driving Doctor'. The Daily Telegraph, for whom he writes weekly safer driving columns, even dares to refer to him as 'God's Chauffeur'.

The world's leading manufacturers, 'blue chip' companies, law firms and private individuals alike, trust his expert knowledge and wealth of experience on driving matters.

He was recently awarded the prestigious Prince Michael *Special* Road Safety Award for his contribution to the specialist driver training industry.

Paul's vast experience, reputation and awesome driving talent make him the ideal person to write on the subject of the 'expert driver'.

Peter Amey is a retired police superintendent, chief driving instructor and examiner.

Early in his career he became a Class 1 police driver.

By the mid 1970s Peter had become an instructor at the South East Regional Police Driving School at Maidstone, involved in driver training and teaching law and vehicle mechanics.

In 1978 he attended a one year post graduate teacher training course at London University.

In 1979 he was appointed for two years to the staff of the Home Office Instructor Training Unit in Harrogate as a Director of Studies on police instructors' courses.

By 1985, now as a chief inspector, he was appointed the chief instructor and examiner in charge of the SE Regional Police Driving School, responsible for all standard level and advanced courses.

During the late 1980s Peter became concerned at the growing number of accidents involving police vehicles, particularly in pursuit situations. He carried out a research project that led him to believe that a new approach to driver training was required. As a result he began to work towards updating the police methods of driver training and, in particular, the police publication 'Roadcraft'. He submitted papers to police conferences, published articles in national magazines, gave lectures throughout the country and even appeared on 'Top Gear'. Eventually the Association of Chief Police Officers agreed that 'Roadcraft' needed updating and commissioned work that led to the manual we have today.

Peter has an academic degree in management and has worked as a consultant to the Kent University Business School. He was also appointed an honorary fellow of the Law School at the University of Kent at Canterbury in 1991.

Peter has always had a passion for cars and motorcycles and has driven/ridden a great variety of vehicles in many different situations. His saddest motoring moment was having to part with a 1934 MG PA restoration project due to lack of money and his most memorable is being given the opportunity to drive the 1920's MG, called 'old number one', in London.

In the early 1990s Peter became acquainted with Sir John Whitmore and Paul Ripley who were also, independently, seeking to update advanced driver training standards and instruction methods. Their association and work on driving standards continues to this day.

Peter Amey and **Paul Ripley** have co-authored this book in an effort to combine their unique range of both teaching and hands-on experience in such a way as to benefit the many others who likewise strive ever to become expert drivers.

What is an Expert Driver?

Have you reached your full potential as a driver?
Have you anything more to learn?
So, are you an expert driver?
Indeed, what is an expert driver?

Perhaps you would consider well-known Formula One racing drivers such as the Schumachers, Alain Prost, Stirling Moss, to be expert drivers?

But are racing drivers good drivers? One must acknowledge their brilliance at racing – but does that make them expert road drivers? We can only guess that they are but we are never told because it is not that for which they are known. They are renowned for their ability to race a car on a circuit with all that that encompasses. They become famous because they are highly skilled at car control whilst driving extremely quickly.

So what do you need to be a good driver on the road?

As with a racing driver you need good car control skills. However, if you were to drive at racing speeds on a road, you would soon be in trouble. So you need to drive at a sensible speed but how do you judge what is sensible and safe? Clearly by looking at and assessing what is happening on the road. These are road skills, which combine many individual techniques, observation and planning, and your previous experience of what is likely to happen on the road.

Does being a skilled driver make you an expert driver? It is certainly a vital part of the whole driving package – but is it enough? Racing drivers certainly have more to offer than just skill to drive very quickly. For example, if their cars are not set up properly, they will not perform to their ultimate potential. For this to be achieved they need knowledge of what is happening to their cars (car feel) and then to be able to communicate this to the engine, chassis and handling engineers. Changes can then be engineered to make the car perform more effectively on the track. So, to become the best, racing drivers have to be experts at test-driving and car feel.

As its driver you need to know what is going on with your car. For example, at a basic level, you need to know what the effect is of changing to a higher or lower gear. At a much higher, 'expert' level, you need to know what are the effects of oversteer and understeer and the relevance of front-, rear- and four-wheel drive in preventing or utilising these effects.

Racing drivers also have intimate knowledge of the rules that apply to driving on a circuit. As some have found to their cost, if they disobey them they will be punished and could lose valuable championship points. Similarly, a good road driver must have up-to-date knowledge of the rules of the road, as laid down in the Highway Code. Disobeying them can endanger other road users, as well as being a means of acquiring penalty points on your licence, or worse.

So we need skills and knowledge – but is that enough? Well, there is one vital ingredient left which even racing drivers can show they lack at times. Skilled and knowledgeable they may be but they can still get themselves involved in accidents if they lose their 'cool' with other drivers, or themselves. To drive safely on the road you must adopt consistently an appropriate attitude. It is so easy from the perceived safety of the driving seat to be aggressive, over-confident, or even to drift into a world of your own! The facts of life are that inappropriate attitudes lead to instances of bad driving and/or confrontational situations and that accidents surely follow.

Will possession of the finest skills, knowledge and a safety-led attitude make you a good driver? Yes – if you can demonstrate that you have highly developed car control and road

Are Formula One drivers complete experts?

---

skills combined with an unerring knowledge and safety-led attitude, then you deserve to be called a good driver.

Being a good driver needs to manifest itself in three main ways. Firstly and most importantly, you have to be super safe; secondly, you must be controlled, smooth and balanced; and thirdly, you must always drive at an appropriate speed for the conditions and circumstances. A good driver aims consistently to remain in the top rank on all three counts.

However, it is in our view, only whilst performance in all three essential disciplines reaches the very highest levels by continued training, dedication and application that drivers can consider themselves 'expert drivers'.

This book sets out how YOU can achieve and then maintain that standard.

Chapter 1:

Road to Expert Driving

How Good Are You?

If we all knew the answer to the question 'What makes a great driver?' there would be no need for a book such as this. You would, as a keen enthusiastic driver, already have achieved that level of driving ability, already have made the grade! Indeed you would have no need for any further advancement of your skills, knowledge or understanding. Nor any need to find out the 'trade secrets', contained in these pages, which are the very essence of a truly expert driver. No – you would be perched at the pinnacle of excellence, 'no more questions', OK!

In such a 'perfect' world – we must warn – you would already have the framework of greatness engulfing you, influencing your thoughts, deeds and actions whenever you were behind the wheel. Nothing would phase you or beat you in your elevated feeling of total command of everything great drivers need to have in their armoury of driving talents. In these terms more tuition or guidance become superfluous. You're one of the greatest drivers in the world. You have joined the select few who have mastered these attributes already.

The burning question, however, is whether you have simply become a legend in your own mind. Should you ever succumb to such awesome, euphoric thinking, you need not feel lonely, because you share it with many other drivers.

Danger ensues only when you ignore its unreality or fail to gain from the insight it provides into correct anticipation of poor or appalling driving going on around you – or into which you may be tempted yourself. You must tackle these dangers, whenever they may apply to you, head on.

Reality is what counts in this book. Do you really think that you are not capable of improvement, that you couldn't become a better driver? Are you *that* good? Ask yourself why you consider yourself one of the greatest road drivers ever? Might there just be some cracks in your driving ability that need a little work? Do you always get your speed and course right on bends? Do you assess all overtaking manoeuvres correctly? Do other road users ever remonstrate with you?

Even if you only concede that there is a small element of your skill or ability that would benefit from further coaching or guidance then progress has already been made within your own self-belief. You are on the right track to opening your mind to that of an expert driver. If this book is going to work for you (most certainly it will if you let it!), you will have to be completely honest with yourself. Becoming a much better driver, perhaps even better than you thought possible, depends on it.

Improvement is within everyone but most importantly, within you. This book is designed to access where you can improve your driving and thus raise the standard of your game. How does that sound to you? Are you ready to meet the challenge?

You must be prepared for constructive self-criticism. Only you can decide this. If you are to make progress it is only you who can allow it to play its proper part whilst you consider the state of your driving. You cannot go forward if you do not remain self-critical and reflect on your own driving performance every time you get behind the wheel.

No driver can produce a drive that is even close to perfection. That driver does not exist and never will. Even drivers of extraordinary talent (a rare breed), who can do most things well, still have something that lets them down every time they drive. Thus every single one of us has the capacity to improve our driving further – even the expert driver this book aspires to make of you.

What Makes an 'Expert Driver'?

A burning ambition constantly to assess your own driving abilities, values, beliefs and ego makes a good start – provided always that you can accept along the way all the advice given above.

You must develop this. Being totally content, comfortable and at ease with your current driving ability and standards is what might otherwise stop you improving. This is what usually stops average drivers from taking the next steps forward to becoming good drivers and prevents good drivers from reaching the next stage – becoming expert drivers. Having an over-inflated or unrealistic opinion of your driving prowess (as discussed earlier) also stops you from progressing, irrespective of where you are on the stepladder of driving ability.

Given ambition and commitment, however, you can improve – beyond your wildest dreams. You can become an expert driver, one of those who enjoy the respect of their passengers, colleagues and friends. Your family will notice the difference in the way you do things behind the wheel. Your safety, smoothness, temperament and the whole ambience in your car will change. Does that sound good? We hope what we write here will produce just that reward.

We ask you now to delve a little further into what may yet be preventing you individually from reaching that goal.

Time to Reflect

Think about your personal driving for a while. Think back and take a long, hard look at yourself and the way you drive now. You need to reflect how you currently drive in all the different situations you can bring to mind. Evaluate *why* you become frustrated with other drivers, if you do, *why* perhaps you sometimes lose your cool and are even tempted to 'take it out' on them. Think about what makes you lose your temper and feel that instant urge to retaliate or remonstrate.

Such emotions are natural enough. What matters is that your subsequent reactions remain under your control. So, you must work on *why* you may sometimes be allowing your emotions to get on top of you, *why* you can fail immediately to grasp the greater good of forgiveness and safety. Perhaps your blood boils when you make a mistake and get hooted. You may lack the confidence of knowing what to do next. Why does everyone else on the road seem to be 'getting at you'?

Ask yourself whether expert drivers would let such things dent their equilibrium. 'No' is the definite answer! Then probe the differences between you and them. What responses might they have at their fingertips that are eluding you? This is your first priority – to look at yourself and the way you go about your driving, and compare it with the way experts perform. So, wherein lies the difference?

The Key to Improvement

If you were told that there was one, single quality in your driving that could make you as much as eighty five per cent safer and better than you are currently, you would surely be intrigued. There is. This factor has little to do with pure driving technique. Its focus, rather, is upon the relative excellence among drivers of the safety-led driving attitude to which we referred in our Introduction.

It may come as a shock to learn the truth, which is that perfecting your safety-led attitude is, without question, the most potent force in your driving make-up. We believe its importance places all other desirable driving attributes in the shade. So few British drivers appear to be 'on message' here that we can be pretty sure their lack of understanding is the major symptom holding back improvements in our driving standard. Consider also the infinite damage that conflicting attitudes to a safety-led one can inflict.

Your target, therefore, is to build a brilliant, safety-led driving attitude. Ours is to enable you to develop this; because your ability to do so is what will absolutely control how you progress in becoming an expert driver. Ultimately, you want to acquire the art of *live* self-assessment, monitoring your own safety-led attitude in real time, as you drive, against the benchmark of perfection.

Chapter 2:

Correct Mental Approach

Who? Me?

Understanding your mental approach to driving is vital. The major divisions are between your 'attitude' and your 'state of mind'. Your attitude takes time gradually to change whereas your state of mind can change hour by hour and day by day. Although your underlying attitude largely dictates your mental approach towards driving, your state of mind can also exert a considerable influence. For example, aggressive drivers who lack much insight will probably always be aggressive, but they will be less so when in a good mood and more so when upset or angry.

Attitude

A correct attitude enhances other learning and experience, whereas poor attitude swiftly overrides the effects of good technical training and often with serious consequences. You can spend a lot of time and effort honing your skills and knowledge but, for example, if your attitude towards feeling tired while driving is to ignore it and drive on regardless, an accident may well result. Many accidents are caused by poor mental control. Your attitude profoundly affects your thoughts, actions and reactions in subtle as well as obvious ways.

   A distinction needs to be made between the attitudes you display fairly consistently in your life, such as passion, passivity, anxiety, or impatience; and the attitude you must adopt when you are in the driving seat. As a pedestrian you are probably, by and large, polite to other people and even quick to apologise if you accidentally bump into someone else. But what are you like behind the wheel? Remember we wrote that you have to be completely honest with yourself. That includes whilst reading this book!

What happens if another driver inconveniences you? Do you swear, blast your horn, or maybe just simmer inside and mutter to yourself? Have you ever thought why otherwise normal people are apt to behave so aggressively at the wheel? Is it perhaps because of a feeling that they are one step removed from the possibility of verbal or physical confrontation? The larger and beefier the car, the greater it seems can be the feeling of security from attack – as if the driver were clad in automotive armour!

For example, with main road traffic queuing and you waiting at a minor road to join it, haven't we all come across the character who, with never a sideways glance, moves up close

Why do people tend to behave so aggressively when placed inside a car?

behind the car in front so as to block off your opportunity to enter the traffic stream in front of him? He may have a hell of a life or a hell of a partner, but it is more probable when removed from his car that he is an ordinary, decent person. Are you like that? Before you suggest 'never', answer yourself this: how often have you let someone into the queue in front of you and felt good about it, yet nonetheless subscribe to the view, 'God help anyone who pushes in uninvited!'?

Attitudes only tend to change slowly but various events can bring about improvements. For example, attitudes towards 'green' issues remained fairly static for years; however, large media attention has caused a considerable change in people's attitudes to all things 'green'. Indeed, an increasing number of people consider the environmental impact of the car they decide to purchase.

Being totally honest, is your driving attitude appropriate? Has a trusted friend remarked unfavourably on your driving attitude? Accepting that you need to identify that part of your driving attitude which is having so profound an effect is the only reaction you can have which may help you change for the better.

Attitudes shift as a consequence of horror. For example, involvement in a serious accident can forever change your attitude towards driving. However, the experience does not need to be that dramatic provided it makes you think.

How would you deal with a taxi driver who pulls out in front of you and causes you to make an emergency stop? You might be so incensed as to get out and shout at him but what if he waits for you to calm down and then politely says, 'I'm really sorry; but haven't you ever made a mistake?' We suggest it would probably disarm you and reduce your anger – although, of course, you may by now feel more vulnerable having got out of the car! Once you begin to think about what the taxi driver said it could well have a permanent effect on your own attitude. You may just become more tolerant in the future when you realise that, inevitably, sometimes you will be as much in the wrong as he was.

Involvement in a serious accident can forever change your attitude towards driving!

Much as we all would like to be considerate to others on the road we are all subject to human error with all the frailties that that involves. The ideal is that there should be no limits to consideration but who doesn't fall far short of this?

You can improve matters immediately if you begin to view traffic movement, especially where traffic is heavy, as a flow; much the same as you see with an army of ants travelling to and from their anthill. Despite their large numbers the ants flow freely because of their mutual understanding and purpose. As driver, your job is to move in, within, and out of the flow of traffic causing the minimum of disruption and upset to others. Everyone then benefits, including you. Approach your relative progress in traffic competitively and you will inevitably upset others, as well as yourself. There is little to gain anyway and, by disrupting the flow with aggressive intrusions, you may actually slow it down. However, keep in mind that dawdling can unleash others' anger too; so try consciously to avoid causing a line of traffic behind.

Once you adopt this attitude of maintaining the flow, things like road positioning, when and where to signal, when to yield and when to close up all become rather obvious. There is a collective purpose; a mutual venture in which other road users become tacit partners and co-operation is the game. You can even draw satisfaction from controlling your anger when others err, because this prevents you from losing concentration, making more mistakes yourself or making worse any problem already caused.

Watch for motorcycles moving up between lines of traffic and give them room to get past. (An expert driver should never be surprised being overtaken by motorcyclists passing up between lanes, even when his own lane has drawn to a halt. It's a tough standard is keeping awake!) Keep rolling at filter junctions wherever possible. Where traffic systems merge, you should dovetail together in the order that best enhances traffic flow, rather than 'insist' on a particular turn. Always use your mirrors *before* you act so as to avoid potential disruption behind.

In the country, especially, continually adjust your speed to the road configuration and other vehicles by watching a long way ahead, thereby almost eliminating the need to use your brakes. This way your every brake pedal touch won't start a chain reaction behind or, conversely, find itself ignored. Make your intentions abundantly clear to other road users by being consistent in terms of speed and positioning and giving clear signals.

None of these little things you can do automatically to help the flow and maintain your own mental equilibrium as you drive are particularly virtuous, generous, or clever, nor do they require any undue effort. Our brief list here is just to introduce you to the sort of adjustments you can continue to think of making to your driving to help smooth the way for yourself and everyone else.

We do not suggest that you should adopt a mechanistic set of prescribed courtesies; we simply ask you to view other road users as worthy of kindness and consideration. Appropriate driving behaviour should then arise almost without effort out of your natural feelings for them. It is for you to ensure nothing ever undermines this courtesy principle. In time and with practice your tolerance towards others will improve and you will be better able to deal with the shortcomings they may have.

Fear plays quite a large role in some drivers' attitudes and behaviour. They can be afraid of everything from other traffic to rain, fog and large lorries. Their tentativeness, slowness and tendency to brake suddenly for no apparent reason make them a liability to themselves and others. Some become so wrapped up in concern for themselves, or so overwhelmed by the situation, that they are then apparently oblivious to the problems they cause others.

If you find fears are controlling your driving in any way, it's time to investigate how to cope when similar circumstances prevail. Consider reading, especially about the Rules of the Road, taking training and specific practice which, between them, should alleviate such fears. Fear breeds on ignorance. Knowledge melts it away.

States of Mind

Expert drivers recognise that their attitude is affected by their state of mind. One day you wake up feeling good, the next you start in a bad mood. If you are generally placid, a foul mood will tend to make you less patient, a good mood more patient. But your temper can change quickly. A bad exchange with your boss can swing contentment to indignation in seconds, with consequent adverse effects immediately compromising your safety-led driving attitude.

Some states of mind are thankfully beneficial to driving, just as some are dangerous but we are all subject to them. The following are perhaps the most common factors which influence your state of mind when driving:

Concentration

Most of us probably associate concentration with trying hard rather than succeeding, and with stress rather than relaxation. In fact, true concentration calms the butterfly mind. It is a receptive state in which information is assimilated, mainly through the senses. Concentration can focus attention on one point – for example, on the ball in tennis or, as in driving, on a quick, automatic, and wide ranging process that is both desirable and easily achievable.

Urged to concentrate more when behind the wheel, you may respond by trying harder to do everything right. This can produce the appearance of correct behaviour, yet be a million miles from true concentration. The excessive effort is stressful and as such may result in further mistakes.

The relaxed concentration you must instead seek is achieved through interest, not by force. Notice how you never have to be told to watch the television screen if the programme is sufficiently interesting. It follows that the secret of maintaining a high degree of attention on your driving is to develop a greater interest on the factors needed in doing so – by reading this book, for example.

Excessive instruction and resulting rigidity of action can actually detract from this keen interest. Your brain addresses its memory for advice first, instead of instantly reacting appropriately to new relevant information as it is happening. To the extent that your memory-processing focus may be unnecessary, your reaction times can be severely slowed.

Strangely, diverting an anxious mind away from worrying excessively about absolute driving correctness usually improves performance. Unfortunately, it is often hard for already nervous drivers to be persuaded that reducing their attention on some aspects of their driving will not make things worse. Their overriding concern has become whether they can cope adequately with *all* the things that they believe they have to think of *at once* in order to drive safely. So a deliberate downgrading of some of these would seem to them to be a recipe for disaster.

Encouragement that this need not be so demands explanation. What needs to be achieved is not to silence completely the parts of the mind that do the driving but to damp down the knowing, critical, chattering voice in the head that does not trust the driving part, takes it over, blocks logical thought taking place in situ, and causes mistakes to be made. Good driving takes over directly this anxiety is switched off. For example, a motorway novice may fret that he will miss vital lane changes where two motorways on his route diverge. Lorries may obscure unexpectedly complex, text signpostings while speed further inhibits their readability. Yet this worry can be all but eliminated by locating the right junction number concerned from a map before setting off. These numbers occupy the same position on all motorway sign gantries around Britain and therefore there is no need for him to read more than this number on any other junction sign before he reaches the one in question. Approaching that junction he can then multiply the gap ahead of him sufficiently by letting those ahead draw further away, to give plenty of time to select the required lane.

Knowing how to tackle the problem in advance allows all the anxiety to fall away, leaving the brain free to interpret the direction instruction correctly in a state of calm confidence.

The focus on real priorities stops these being crowded out by lesser ones at the critical time. In this simple example, the person concerned would probably discover, having absorbed the priority information, that he then had time to read the rest of those signs anyway!

Relaxation

Although relaxation is a beneficial state, one in which you feel good and perform well, few of us have ever been taught how to relax. Even fewer can relax on demand. When ordered to relax you tend to feel even more tense. Unfortunately relaxation is usually not something that can be readily turned on and off at will. Though we may acknowledge it as our natural, passive state, we also know how easily it can be disrupted by anxieties and fears.

Relaxation is boosted when you are able to put aside anxieties and fears. In your daily life, you will have noticed how your level of relaxation varies as the degree of outside interference increases or decreases. For example, you may feel relaxed until you have to deal with a difficult customer but you will calm down again when you go to the canteen for a coffee break. It is important to recognise the extent that your level of relaxation is affected by what is going on within your everyday thinking. Simply recalling that difficult customer can trigger a further loss of relaxation.

Much can be done to reduce the effects of these influences whilst driving. When you practise becoming more aware of what is going on within yourself and how that bears upon your driving performance, you will be encouraged to root out the causes of any nervousness. The substitution of know-how, where formerly ignorance may have played havoc, will effectively shut out most of the disturbing thoughts. For example, extreme fear of icy conditions can be reduced to normal caution within an hour or so on a proper skid-pan. See Appendix.

Expert drivers are always relaxed at the wheel. They adjust the driving seat to fit like a mould and sit back comfortably, without compromising their light but firm steering wheel hold. Their movements over the controls are minimal, fluid, unhurried and purposeful. The calm confidence exuded by such drivers is conveyed unspoken to their passengers.

These are the observable characteristics of a driver who is relaxed. Emulation of them at the wheel will not itself of you a relaxed driver make; for relaxation comes from the inside out, not the outside in. However, the adoption of such outward signs of expertise can undoubtedly help to evoke genuine relaxation in your driving.

Stress

Inability to relax leads to stress, and then other negative states of mind and attitudes are accentuated. Stress may arise out of an immediate situation such as heavy traffic causing you to worry about being late for an appointment. It may surface every time you step into your car because you are afraid of having an accident or it may only become a problem when one of your children is in the car. Many unfortunate people are chronically anxious or stressed about issues that have nothing to do with their driving. Regrettably, that will take its toll on their driving also.

Regardless of the root cause, stress and tension seriously impair the performance, safety and pleasure of driving. Striving to remove stress without knowing how is inclined to make it worse. The right way forward is to become more aware about what you feel and do, and to bring into play a very clear resolve about the state you want to move towards. Shortly, in this chapter we will return to explain some self-awareness techniques which can dramatically improve your mental approach to driving.

Fatigue

Fatigue leads to loss of concentration, drowsiness and the horrific danger of falling asleep at the wheel. There is no shadow of doubt that driving very long distances without appropriate breaks, particularly on motorways, causes fatigue.

There is little to alleviate the condition other than to take rest. The trouble is the effects are cumulative. Opening the windows, stopping for coffee and other techniques may help for a short while but, inevitably, fatigue will again take over until satisfactory rest is taken. Considerable willpower is required to break or postpone a journey but it is the only safe course of action when facing mounting fatigue.

Anger

Anger soon results in irrational, risky or aggressive driving which one may or may not live to regret. Anger can be carried onto the road by circumstances that have occurred away from the car, for example, from domestic problems at home. On other occasions it comes whilst in the car, for example, by the reaction to another driver's actions. It is worth remembering that few such actions are deliberate and that you yourself have made your fair share of mistakes but such rational thought is seldom available in the heat of the moment. Explicit criticism of other road users by mouthing oaths or rude gesticulations from within a car say more about your own inadequacy than that of the person at whom you direct it. People under stress, like those in a mad dash who hurry because they have not left enough time for their journey, or those with a competitive/ aggressive attitude towards their fellows – it ought to go without saying – are far more susceptible to outbursts of anger on the road.

Distractions

There are many potential distractions on the road, from the activities of pedestrians, to shop windows. Taking a keener interest in all the skills of your driving will reduce or eliminate the diversionary effect of such tempting attractions. This is the only road to go. Ironically, one of the most irresistible distractions is the aftermath of a road accident, which all too often results in delays caused by gauping motorists. Some distractions emanate from within the car such as unruly children; others are self-inflicted such as mobile phones, arguments with a passenger, or trying to eat or drink at the wheel.

Distractions are not excuses for errors. It is up to you to eliminate them (e.g. mobile phones, eating and drinking) or manage them legally and safely.

Mental Health

The ability to drive can be severely affected by mental health problems. These illnesses can only be addressed by qualified medical practitioners and our advice cannot replace that treatment. Furthermore, the over-confidence or extreme excitement of mania, whether inherent in the personality or drug- or alcohol-induced, momentary or prolonged, is deadly in the driving seat.

Awareness

So, in our analysis, the critical parts of becoming an expert driver lie in holding the right attitude and maintaining an appropriate state of mind. Fine, but how do you develop this correct mental approach? The key starting point is to improve your self-awareness. If you begin to think hard about what you are doing and always consider the consequences of your actions on others as well as yourself, your mental approach will gradually fall into line. Indeed, we can assure you that, in time, your attitude will change to such a degree that self-awareness becomes second nature to your driving.

One of the great benefits of this is the way that you will find it enables you to hone your skills. You learn better to translate into skilled car handling the messages that the car is sending you through the controls and the 'seat of your pants'.

So many aspects of awareness appear throughout this book, you must forgive us for defining here at some length what can be meant by it.

Awareness is the general description given to the simultaneous consciousness of all the information currently coming in from your senses. To raise awareness is to gather at once more detailed and complete information from your senses than normal. To focus your awareness is to concentrate your attention on one sense or on one aspect of what is going on. Awareness is most usually concerned with your experience of what is happening in the present as distinct from your thoughts about what went on in the past or your ideas on what to do next.

There are two forms of awareness: being aware of things outside your body and being aware of what is going on inside. Athletes and dancers develop a high degree of sensitivity to the insides of their bodies. Not unexpectedly, they call this 'listening to the body'. Masseurs and sculptors learn to achieve a highly skilled sense of touch. Sensitivity and ability tend to develop in parallel so, for example, excelling at a sport or music will impart in you a more sensitive use of your body or hands. In turn, you find yourself more able – a better athlete, dancer, trampolinist, or whatever.

Thus it is that reaching a high degree of awareness about yourself and your driving ability enables you to take significant strides forward both in your mental approach and your skill levels.

Self-Assessment

To ensure the development of self-awareness you need to employ self-assessment techniques. Once established, you never discard them; they must become a part of your driving.

So how do you go about self-assessment? You ask yourself the following questions:

---

a)   WHAT DID I NOTICE ABOUT THAT SECTION OF MY DRIVING?

b)   HOW DID IT AFFECT OTHER ROAD USERS?

For example, although negotiating a busy town centre on a Saturday morning may require concentrated effort for some time, at the end you may find it difficult to recall more than one or two highlights about which you had to make choices and which therefore are worthy of further consideration. The important thing is not the number of items but that you do make the effort to do this. Thus, in this instance, you might have noticed a feeling of impatience towards a driver in front of you who seemed to be going too slowly or perhaps because he became distracted too readily. You may also consider, looking back, that you communicated this impatience by driving too close to the slow vehicle. How did your driving affect your passengers – did it unsettle them too?

On an advanced driving course your instructor should be asking you these questions and encouraging you to ask them of yourself. One of the great aids in police driver training is the encouragement to be self-critical and to discuss a section of driving with your crew member(s). Indeed the habit starts on driving courses but becomes part of the culture in the patrol car – thus leading to continued awareness and development.

The exact format of the questions you ask yourself matters less than that you get into the habit of questioning how you have just driven and also how it affected other road users, including any passengers in your car. It may be that these questions need to be asked after only one manoeuvre. For example, immediately following a series of bends, you should briefly assess how well you judged your speed and position.

Your answers and the improvements they should foreshadow will stack up in your subconscious ready to cut out repetitive errors.

Usually something will have been less than perfect and, by recognising it, the next similar situation will provide an opportunity to improve. You will soon begin to adapt the questions to the situation. For example, in respect of your line through those bends: 'Did my manoeuvre alarm others? Did it confuse them (ahead, approaching or behind)? Did someone need to take avoiding action? Did I cause someone to brake? Was my hand position awkward? Was I in the right gear throughout? How was my road positioning? Would my speed – judged realistically – have allowed me to stop within the distance I could see to be clear at every stage?' In general terms you will really be asking yourself *'How could I have improved my driving there?'*

Asking yourself such questions seems quite a long process when written on these pages. In reality, it takes only a second or two. You will raise your skills of observation, recognising potential hazards and planning rapidly once you get in the swing of it. And doing so will boost your mental control.

Before long such awareness-raising self-interrogation becomes automatic, subconscious and an integral part of your driving. As we leave this subject, we should emphasize that becoming self-aware has proved to be one of the finest and quickest ways of improving drivers' attitudes and abilities.

Chapter 3:

Observation

Enhanced observation stems naturally from increased awareness. But you need more than just seeing what comes in your
immediate line of vision. You need to scan systematically to
ensure you gain all the information available. How well you
then assess its value will determine the quality of your planning and of your revisions to that during what will often be a
rapidly changing outlook.

An expert behind the wheel continuously appraises what he
sees and needs to know about the road ahead and relates it to
his experience. He adds to that picture both what his mirrors
reflect and regular coverage of what is (or may shortly be)
alongside him on either side. The combined whole is what he
uses to govern his selection of a safe speed and position
moment-to-moment.

As with most other good drivers, you will see him stop
gently at red traffic lights or to allow passage to those on foot
at pedestrian crossings. You will note his correct early selection
of lane at junctions and so on. But the BIG difference, which
you may only detect as your own driving standard rises, will be
in the infinite pro-active changes he makes to his position
and/or speed as the degree of danger affecting his path constantly rises or subsides. Many of his alterations will be fractional and hard to spot. However, a prime way to single him
out is to watch his behaviour when the going gets tough. He
does not 'get going'; that's for sure! For example, in a particular brief stretch, within a long speed-restricted area, the pave-
ments might be swarming with shoppers on both sides,

narrowing all escape options were one of them to step or stumble off the kerb. A maximum, safe speed past them might be 15 mph, or even 5 mph if approaching traffic also wants to squeeze through. Then the expert will drop speed under those maxima, covering his brake pedal as well through the most critical stage. He won't continue at a brain-dead, break-neck 30 or 40 mph!

On the contrary, what you recognise most, once you place him under the closest scrutiny, are his never-ending, safety-led adjustments to what is going on all around him. The degree of variation in his approach, already notably higher than that of others, will be most marked when he is intent on making swift progress.

We started this chapter by saying the expert accounts not

An expert will extract every detail from this scene – can you?

just for what he sees but for what he 'needs to know' about the road ahead. We can now break this observation down into its constituent parts:

a)   Road Layout

Many drivers fail to assess rapidly enough the continuously moving point on the road ahead where their view of it unfolds. As a result, they are beset with making last-second decisions. This matters a lot as you approach bends, hill crests and, even more, hidden dips. You must not only be aware of what is immediately in front of you but also of what stretches out in the mid-foreground and the long distance. If a tricky junction on your route is seen in good time, you can adjust your speed and position until you know that no one can (or might) swing across your path. An early look at a bend gives you time to assess its severity and plan your entry speed accordingly. Assessing a bend accurately depends on practice and experience but your skill develops much more quickly if you arrive better prepared.

b)   Other Traffic

There is traffic you can see and traffic that you cannot see but which may be there. An example of the latter might be a low sports car concealed by hedgerows at the tricky junction above.

Remember, human beings may be quite unpredictable. Therefore, when you see another vehicle arriving at or waiting at such a junction (including any hoping to turn right from the opposite direction to yours), you must assess what its driver may do next. If he stays where he is there is no problem but you must be prepared to do what you can to minimise the danger should he move out of turn.

If a vehicle could be hidden there, you must take similar care.

If the road in the opposite direction happens to be entirely clear, you may be able to pull a little towards the crown-of-the-road. This can yield earlier vision of a blind side road to your left and greater manoeuvrability if things go wrong but the concept must never be abused; for example, crossing a hazard centre line is rarely acceptable.

You may imagine you have made eye contact with such a driver. His position/speed may likewise offer you confidence he won't make some mistake. But it is just when you least expect them that the big accidents happen! When you correctly anticipate error, position wisely, have speed in check and cover your brake as suggested above, the chances are you will avoid a smash. It is precisely when you have made (incorrect) assumptions and/or taken little or no such precautions that he pulls across your bows without apparently having even seen you.

Sometimes, although you presumed he saw you when looking your way, his gaze will not have had you in focus or you will have been in a blind spot when looked at from his viewing position. On other occasions, his brain may say 'go!' when it means the opposite – wait! (Have you never carried out the exact opposite of what you intended? It's a normal, human trait, although thankfully, a very infrequent one.) Or it may have committed him to 'go!' too late to reverse his decision. No matter; more fool you, we are bound to write, if you hit him.

c)   **Pedestrians**

You need to plan for anyone on foot to do the unexpected, particularly children and, to a lesser degree, the elderly. Remember that pedestrians can change direction much quicker than vehicles. Someone walking along a pavement can turn and walk into the road in an instant. Fortunately, adults at least normally give some indication such as a quick glance and, if this is observed, early avoiding action can be taken.

d)   **Road Signs and Markings**

Few drivers consider these sufficiently at all. Partly, this is because our roads are littered with a huge excess of signs, many of them boringly repetitive. This deprives those that really matter of having much beneficial effect. The expert driver nonetheless takes pride in noting every grain of information that signs and markings foretell. Some more interesting examples follow in no particular order:

1.   A change from lane-divider lines to hazard lines warns you that something about the road ahead requires your attention. Yet many drivers do not even seem to know there is any difference between the two types of line. The expert loves the challenge of spotting whatever it may be, at the earliest opportunity.

Our roads are littered with a huge excess of signs!

2.   Temporary signs are perhaps ignored even more than most, probably due to a large extent by their retention after hazards have long since been cleared. However, when you see a road works sign, for example, you dare not ignore it and not slow down, because round the next

bend may be an obstruction. It is annoying if the road works have already disappeared but you must never risk this. The next one you see may really indicate road works.

3.   An expert picks up many clues about the shape of junctions and user priorities from direction signs – which other drivers see only as denoting the way to this or that destination.

e)   **Positioning for View**

You can greatly enhance how much you see by astute positioning. Experience and thought will be your guides if you consciously try to improve your view by positioning your vehicle well. For example, the distance you can see around a bend to the left may be unnecessarily restricted if you keep too close to the nearside. Try lining up a little further out and see how much further you can see round the bend. Oncoming traffic, or the threat thereof, must restrict how far you decide it's sensible to move out but a safe balance should easily be achieved – always subject to what your mirrors may be telling you or the presence of anyone alongside. See overleaf.

In a similar way, for a bend to the right, a line well to your left usually offers improved vision. Again a balance must be struck because such a movement may, for instance, restrict your view past a lorry you are following or risk collision with a cyclist it is passing. Indeed, it may even unwittingly encourage a driver behind you to think that you would like him to overtake you.

On a crowded motorway, a pinch to the left or right of the exact line of the vehicle you are next behind should scarcely affect your closeness to drivers alongside you, but may open your long view ahead by dozens of vehicles. This applies especially on very straight motorways, where leaving yourself an extra couple of car lengths between you and it will also redouble the benefit of this 'Positioning for View' technique again. On curvy motorways, you can afford to be a little closer as the bends themselves open up your forward view.

Again, in heavy motorway traffic choose, where you can, to follow low-slung vehicles (at a respectable distance!) rather

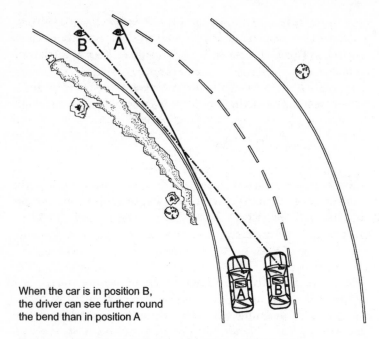

When the car is in position B,
the driver can see further round
the bend than in position A

Correct positioning can enhance your view round a bend

than high-sided vans, coaches or lorries. The enhanced vision this creates enables you to react to danger way out ahead and, hopefully, before any necessity for emergency action can crunch right back to your place in the stream.

f) Road Surfaces

Motorcyclists become more 'street-wise' than car drivers because their survival depends so much on it. But surface awareness is vital study for car drivers too. Road surfaces vary in construction and states of repair. Very worn or polished surfaces provide minimal friction, especially when wet, and demand well-reduced speeds. Most out-of-the-ordinary problems are caused by oil, ice, mud, wet leaves and other such deposits on the surface. Mostly, you can spot those in time and plan accordingly, although diesel spillages can catch you unaware.

Black ice, on the other hand, is almost impossible to see. Is the temperature below freezing? If so, does it look wet – which may be evidence of salting? Dangerously, wetness can turn out to be water sitting on top of ice. When icy blasts are around in freezing conditions, test suspect surfaces with a light touch on your brakes every so often, taking care to do so only when travelling at very slow speed. With luck, you'll rumble the danger before it rumbles you. Stopping distances can multiply by ten times in icy conditions.

g)   Vision and Speed

The knack of flicking your focus between the long, middle and short of the view ahead must become the subject of rigorous, conscious self-training if, for you, it is not already. As your speed increases, so the necessity for you to pay far greater attention further ahead vastly increases in importance. Longer observation improves planning and avoids rushing into situations.

Its value on motorways cannot be over-estimated.

In conditions where driving fast is safe, doing so can only remain so, provided you are constantly at-the-ready to slash speed (and do) at the merest hint of congestion ahead. On motorways, watch not only vehicles ahead; look for tell-tale signs that the spaces between them may be tightening. If they are, react. Judge by the overall weight of traffic too: too heavy, too closely packed; these symptoms dictate that you hold back *more*, now, from whatever may be immediately ahead.

h)   Peripheral Vision

The human eye not only sees forwards but quite a surprising distance sideways as well. We react very quickly to movements in our peripheral vision and that draws our attention to what is happening. You can improve on this by casting regular sideways glances fitted in between essential looking ahead and paying attention to your mirrors.

In summary, keep your eyes moving. Never allow them to 'dwell' on immaterial things. Try to develop a systematic eye-balling approach that prioritises where to look, and when, so that you are always able to cover what matters most. Whenever you feel uneasy that your coverage may be slipping – SLOW DOWN!

Highway Hypnosis

Eyes glazed, looking exclusively at the back of the vehicle immediately ahead is a common, highly dangerous fault. Before you know it, you merely parrot the driver in front, get up too close and lose touch with anticipating necessary changes in speed and direction. You risk finding yourself part of a multiple pile-up. You can even find yourself stopping because the driver of the vehicle ahead decides to park! Such hypnotic attachment to the rear end of the vehicle in front happens more easily at night, when its rear light clusters draw your eyes towards them. It can take considerable willpower to stop this happening to you.

Fortunately there are plenty of ways to prevent it. The first priority, unless intending to overtake, is to stay further back.

You can take advantage of curves to snatch glances beyond bulky vehicles and you can even gain glimpses ahead through the rear window of most cars. Houses, trees or telegraph poles beside the road may foretell bends in the road. The speed of oncoming traffic may provide clues whether there is an open road ahead or if it is slow, tortuous, or obstructed. All these visual tricks of the trade can help keep you safe at all times, and they can be of particular benefit prior to overtaking. However, because of the fleeting nature of such glances, be advised that confirmation of what you originally saw may well be essential.

Other Good Clues

People waiting at bus stops on the other side of the road may indicate a bus shortly approaching – useful knowledge on winding country routes. Fresh deposits of horse dung smell of horses on the road ahead. A freshly cut grass bank, or hedge cuttings swirling about, raise the question – 'Is there a tractor round the next corner?' A racing bicycle 'asks' – 'Are there more strung out ahead?' The clock strikes three (pm) and you need to be thinking – 'Are there children about?'

Mirrors

Remember the purpose of looking in any driving mirror is to see, assess and understand what is going on behind – it is not merely to conform to a ritual. An expert driver monitors his mirrors all the time but probably without any too rigid structure. He just always knows what is going on behind.

The Highway Code urges that a mirror check be made before *any* manoeuvre. That includes unusual acceleration, as well as slowing down before a hazard or deviating from your present route. The latter reinforces common sense because, if you are going to your left or right, you might be moving into space about to be taken by another vehicle. Deviation must therefore include changing lanes, as well as turning itself.

Your mirrors' information always has to come first so that you can gauge the need for an appropriate signal (insofar as those behind may be concerned) and whether it will be safe to do what you intend.

How often you need to make regular mirror checks depends on your judgment in the light of what is happening on the road at the time and the type of road you are travelling on. It is a mistake to suggest that mirror checks should be religiously made at pre-ordained intervals because you could well end up looking in your mirror(s) when a situation in front temporarily demands total concentration. Thus, when driving faster than the average vehicle on an open road, fewer mirror checks may suffice than would be necessary when driving in a suburban area.

Observation Generally

There is a vast, continually changing range of information available to you from outside your car. It is for you to assess what matters and prioritise your actions/reactions accordingly. As with mirror use, an expert driver will not necessarily have to keep checking everything consciously. He will monitor all the key items automatically, cross-reference them, draw conclusions, and react as and when appropriate. This will be a continuous, automatic and largely subconscious activity. However, this level of expertise is rarely reached without long practice and application.

What is Really Happening?

It is one thing to take in what is happening all around you; but how you continually match your driving to suit those ever-shifting circumstances is quite another. For example, if you follow a vehicle which is signalling right and about to pass a lorry parked opposite a road junction, how do you know whether that vehicle simply intends to overtake or whether it is genuinely about to turn right? You have seen all there is to see but experience demands that you plan for either eventuality. Knowledge of similar situations witnessed previously usually enables you to judge the most likely outcome. The length of time its indicators are on and precisely when they are switched on or off provide the sort of clue(s) that may help foretell what is likely to happen. The driver's positioning and speed, however, may turn out to be more reliable indicators.

Perception improves in the light of experience. Unfortunately too many drivers fail to apply lessons learned. They continue to be 'last-second decision artists', devoid of all the advantages which that knowledge should unleash to allow consistent thinking and planning; advantages which must include correct assessment way out ahead of what happens just in front of their very eyes.

Eyesight

Your observation levels will never be good if you have an uncorrected eyesight defect. Most people, however, pass the basic eyesight requirements when they take their driving tests but are rarely tested again until later in life – usually when they notice a difficulty in reading or watching the television. Surprisingly eyesight standards are not subject to checking in the various advanced tests carried out throughout the country.

Thus it remains for individuals to arrange suitable, periodic eyesight tests through their lives. We suggest that you should have a test by a qualified optometrist/optician on a regular basis to ensure that your eyesight is good enough for driving. If you are lucky enough still to enjoy uncorrected vision by age forty, ophthalmic surgeons inform us that annual testing is advisable thereafter, because of the high onset of measurable deterioration that tends to happen within a few years of that

Parked lorry

Is the car indicating to turn right or to pass the lorry?

Can you tell what are this driver's intentions?

age. If your vision for driving needs correction by glasses or contact lenses, it is an offence not to wear these when driving. Police, incidentally, can require you to undertake an eyesight test at any time in good daylight; so you risk your licence as well if irresponsible.

Chapter 4:

Planning

Planning can be either conscious or subconscious. Subconscious planning derives from experience – which therefore has to come first. However, planning will not improve unless conscious effort is made. Planning skill can only develop alongside a safety-led attitude, increased awareness borne of self-assessment and keenly prioritised observation. For example, when you reassess a previous part of your driving, you will, on occasion, have to accept that you rushed into a situation and reacted at the last minute. Such experience should force your planning decisions forward. An expert driver decides on speed, position, line and when to be looking where, much, much earlier than most of those around him.

Only as your planning improves will you also begin really to appreciate just why it's so important. Instead of all too frequently running into grief unprepared, adopt the mental process of working out what is likely to happen, and plan accordingly. Quite often you will need more than one plan. Experience enables you to judge what is the most likely course of events and driving accordingly can become your main plan. However, the unexpected does happen and, in particular, other drivers can do some strange things – so you need to be ready. This process is commonly known as paying attention to the 'what if' factor.

Here is an illustration. Imagine you are approaching a crossroads in a town. You are on the major road. A car waits in the minor road to your left but the right is clear. Experience should warn you that, although you have priority, it is possible that the car may pull out in front of you. You have to plan to go through the crossroads safely but you must also plan for evasive action should the other car pull out. Choosing the safest course and speed will involve checking your mirrors and probably aligning your path closer to the centre line of the road than to the other vehicle. You select your speed and how far out in the road may be safe in the context of what your mirrors show, what effect this course may have on any oncoming traffic (and how any such traffic might dictate a slower speed or a course less far out) and what you believe about whether the driver waiting on the left has seen you as well as what he may or may not do. (A learner, for instance, could be more likely to pull forward simply by mistake.)

The less room you are going to have for crash avoidance if he does pull out, the slower you must be; the one must govern the other. So, if you think hard about it, that 'lunatic' driving smack up on your tail also means less room (to save him from shunting your back) and that means go slower still until the potential danger is passed.

As part of your plan in any such tightening conditions, your right foot will probably ease on the throttle and be ready to move over to the brake. Indeed, you may go further and 'cover' the brake pedal just in case. By this planning, you enhance your safety as well as that of all concerned. You increase your safety margin and are ready to respond no matter what happens. In the event of a necessity to stop, covering your brake like this probably chops as much as a staggering 5 car lengths out of the 9 normally needed to stop completely from 40 mph; statistics aside, your chances of averting a crash are probably doubled and if impact there is, it will be very substantially lessened.

Planning also makes your driving smoother and more flowing. For example, when you need to pass a parked car on your nearside, you should never be caught having to pull out at the last moment, unsettling your car and your passengers. Instead, you signal to those behind, if necessary, and then gradually ease out to pass. Oncoming traffic will take notice sooner and any harsh, circular detour transforms to a smooth curve. Should you need to give way, you can stop at the appropriate point on this curve, suitably well back and still inside the centre line of your road, ready to complete the pass equally smoothly once approaching traffic has passed. By starting the manoeuvre so far in advance of the actual need to change position and speed, the expert often finds he can 'time things' on the curve so as to avoid stopping at all.

Overtaking on a motorway should be a similar process. So many drivers close up behind a slow moving vehicle and leave their overtaking to the last minute that this really does need to be spelt out. They finish up either panic braking because they cannot pull out, or endangering the flow in the adjacent overtaking lane as they force their way out. A good driver will observe the slower vehicle earlier, plan his overtake in good time and then execute it with smoothness and safety. An expert driver coming up from further behind will be forming a judgment about whether the driver just described is a panic merchant or a good driver, and will be adjusting his speed and position for either eventuality.

Specific Driving Plans

'Observation and Planning' is a continuous process all the time you are driving. However, when you intend to execute a particular manoeuvre, you need to make a specific **DRIVING PLAN**. The necessary steps are set out in the chart overleaf and discussed below. Flexibility is vital to deal with any changes in road and traffic conditions and may need to be invoked at any stage.

So, although we record the various elements chronologically in our plan here, it does not mean that they are necessarily sequential or mutually exclusive. Generally, you will consider the stages in the order they are presented but, if the specific circumstances make it appropriate to alter the order, then do so you must. Furthermore, the stages will often switch, overlap or continue throughout the process as noted under **Flexibility**.

DRIVING PLAN Consider in sequence unless appropriate to do otherwise		
PRE-CONDITIONS	Safety Legality Consideration	**F** **L** **E** **X** **I** **B** **I** **L** **I** **T** **Y**
INFORMATION	Observation Mirrors Start to plan your strategy	
SIGNAL	Communicate with other road users (including pedestrians) If in doubt, always signal	
POSITION	Maximise safety margins Create space Maximise views Refine your strategy	
SPEED	Throttle reduction and/or braking Correct speed of approach Safe speed to proceed	
GEAR	Correct gear for road speed Vehicle control and balance Maximise response Maximise flexibility	
PROCEED (IF SAFE TO DO SO)	'Go' situation Balanced vehicle condition Accelerate away	
ACKNOWLEDGE	Friendly wave of hand	

For example, when you execute an overtake, your **Position** might need to take account – sometimes more than once – of your effect on others, maximising views, vehicle control, legality and so on.

To demonstrate the value of using specific Driving Plans, we now take in turn a closer look at each vital element on the chart:

Pre-Conditions

Every fresh manoeuvre demands that you take account of three essential pre-conditions:

- Safety
- Legality
- Consideration of your effect on other road users

Safety is the first pre-requisite of all Driving Plans. If your planned manoeuvre is unsafe, or if the circumstances change and make it unsafe, then it must be aborted. Similarly, if what you are planning is going to be illegal, then you must think and plan again. For example, if you are planning an overtake and you see that if you went ahead you would be unable to return to your own side before the start of a double continuous white centre line, then you must hold back. To go on would not only be unlawful and, probably, unsafe, it would be in blatant disregard of the safety-led attitude that lies at the heart of expert driving.

A large part of being an expert driver is being aware of how your actions will affect other road users. If your overtaking could disturb the driver you are passing if he happens to be nervous, plan accordingly. Only overtake once he looks settled and there is plenty of room to give him a wide berth. Such an overtake can be made more difficult or impossible at night if the driver you wish to pass uses only his dipped beam, despite there being no oncoming traffic.

He, for one, is not considering the effect of his driving upon others!

In this event, you may need to move out, when safe, a little earlier than otherwise, so that you can give a brief flash of high beam of your own headlights to see far enough ahead as you decide to go on or hold back. The intention is not to dazzle him in his offside mirror (which shouldn't happen if your flash is brief); it is solely to confirm the road ahead is clear for you to go. If you do, then don't switch to high beam again until you are abreast of him.

Remember the motto – 'Safety, legality, consideration'.

Information

You cannot plan effectively without information. Your eyes need to be 'here, there and everywhere' as we have emphasised but, nonetheless, you must be careful. Avoid rigorously ever letting your attention 'freeze' on just one part of the all round scene or you will miss other vital aspects. Look twice, often; but never gaze solely at one thing – even a serious accident.

You need to get a grip consistently on the *physical features* of the road (junctions, crests, bends, etc.), *other road users* (moving or parked vehicles, pedestrians, cyclists) and on the *conditions* (road surface, weather, your vehicle, you).

As soon as you start to gather information, you will begin to plan your strategy to execute the manoeuvre. You will think about the need for signals, your position, the correct speed, the required gear and your chosen line. As you gather more and more information you will refine these decisions. This process of gathering information and developing your strategy continues all the while you are planning and executing the manoeuvre. If the road/traffic situation changes, then you must respond and adapt your strategy accordingly.

Signal

You need to indicate your intentions to other road users, and that includes pedestrians. For example, if you intend turning into a minor road and pedestrians are waiting on the kerb side to cross, then a signal will enable them to react to your intentions. This is not only safe driving but also courteous. In this instance, though you may have priority to enter the minor road provided they remain on the pavement, pedestrians will, sometimes, nevertheless step off that kerb – either to cross or intending to do so immediately you have passed. Therefore your speed must drop sufficiently – regardless of any theoretical priority you may have or your having correctly signalled – to be able to stop if necessary to avoid hitting someone.

Sometimes, the considerate thing to do in these circumstances is to stop anyway and wait for such people to cross. However, unless all of them are ready to walk across smartly, and no one behind you will be unduly delayed by your kindness, you might conclude that the danger to both you and them, from traffic behind you shunting you forwards, outweighs such helpfulness. Even so, as you continue slowly round into the turning, you must be at-the-ready to stop should any one of them misinterpret your slowness and step out right in front of you.

Always signal early to provide others with time to react – if in doubt always signal. Make sure your positioning and speed themselves communicate with others as unambiguously as possible, as well. Include in your repertoire the astute use of arm signals, brake lights, horn or headlight flash – whenever each of these can add to the information others need and to safety overall.

Position

Always position to maximise both safety margins and views ahead. The trick is to *create space* so that you can plan, prepare and execute specific manoeuvres in safety and that you will always have some room to spare for the unexpected.

As you position your vehicle to maximise your view, you will be able to refine your strategy still further. You will also position your vehicle so that you can move smoothly into your chosen line once you have decided that it is safe to proceed.

Speed (The Critical Element)

To *create space*, speed must inextricably link with position. Slow down for manoeuvres usually by throttle reduction and/or braking. If braking is required, it should be a single, smooth application wherever possible.

When it is necessary, always lose speed ahead of a manoeuvre, rather than while executing it. For example, when cornering, a slow enough entry speed is critical, and timing your arrival at that speed is a mandatory element of the planning process.

Gear

The correct gear relative to road speed is essential for vehicle control and balance. This will be – in normal conditions – the one that, coming up to any manoeuvre, will maximise response and flexibility and your ability to accelerate away as you complete it. At cruising speeds, it will be your highest, fuel-economical gear. On steep descents, you will want the safety of engine-braking control, using a lower gear(s).

In relatively slow manoeuvres, such as turning into a minor road, it is normal to brake and change gear at the same time. Indeed, this becomes essential when the major road is downhill and you need to hold back your speed on the brakes to prevent overshooting your turn.

When slowing towards a bend, you normally only need one downward gear change and should make this after any braking required. However, you can do this *during* braking if you are skilled at the 'heel-and-toe' method explained in Chapter 8 page 138.

If you do change down whilst braking but without using this method – other than at very modest speed as noted above – it is essential to be gentle and smooth with your clutch re-engagement or you will risk a brief skid as well as putting unnecessary strain on the transmission.

When planning an overtaking manoeuvre, it is necessary to

take a lower gear at an early stage, so that you are ready to maximise acceleration past the other vehicle when a safe 'go' situation occurs, and thus to return to your original lane as soon as possible (see Chapter 5 page 68).

Proceed (if safe to do so)

Before carrying out any manoeuvre, you need to be satisfied that it is safe to begin. For example, you may need to hold back for traffic to clear before turning right. Only when you have a safe 'go' situation, do you proceed.

Prior to steering round a bend, you want to be in a position to begin gentle re-acceleration – so as to create a stable and balanced vehicle condition. This you then do, and this balance should be maintained for the – usually – brief period until visibility and road conditions permit further controlled acceleration away. Note, however, that there may be situations when further speed uptake will not be beneficial, for example, when descending a steep hill.

In an overtaking manoeuvre, remember, the decision to proceed should be followed by hard acceleration to make the pass as safe and efficient as possible.

Acknowledge

A friendly wave of the hand, given whilst it can be seen, lets another road user who may have facilitated your progress know his care is appreciated. It costs nothing and spreads good will.

Flexibility

The expert stays flexible when using his Driving Plan. He knows it is crucial to be able to change it when needs must.

For example, on approaching a bend, you will gather information and, from this, decide on how to position for it. You will adjust your speed according to the severity of the bend and the road conditions. You will have the right gear engaged prior to arrival. Everything will hopefully be just right for you to take the bend – your plan, at least, will look perfect. However, what are you going to do if you suddenly notice that, despite a generally dry road surface, farm tractors have covered the road in wet mud from half way round the bend? Clearly you must cut speed before you reach the mud if you are to avert the danger of skidding into oncoming traffic. Though you will already know what's behind (won't you? – see page 43), its proximity may be less important than avoiding that forward risk. So, you will brake instantly, as hard as necessary, with a view to releasing your pedal fully again by the time you reach the mud. Unless you have an ABS (Anti-lock Braking System – see page 126) you may also have to postpone steering, until then, too. Hopefully, you will then manage to negotiate what's left of the bend, using minimal re-acceleration for stability as discussed above, and reach safety still on your own side of the road.

It follows that you must never get locked into a Driving Plan that cannot be revised rapidly.

Nor can you 'tick off' any item just because you've acted upon it already. When planning an overtake, for example, you will be fine-tuning your position and speed throughout. Geared down for zippy acceleration, you position for best advantage as you confirm you are safe to go ahead. Once under way – if it remains clear and you do proceed – positioning and maintaining sufficient acceleration to return to your own side as soon as safely possible are the main considerations that should spring to the forefront of your mind.

Integrating Driving Plans With Your Own Style

When adopting any new technique, it is imperative to practise it in a controlled manner, in safe surroundings. Think through the type of Driving Plan you want to accomplish for each kind of manoeuvre before trying them out individually. This way should ensure that you begin to introduce Driving Plans safely as you build up using the concept.

You will find you tend to slip up at first. No serious driver likes to make mistakes but you cannot learn without occasionally getting it wrong, so do not worry, provided that safety doesn't become an issue. Simply convert such errors into opportunities for learning – through your self-assessment of what went wrong in each instance.

Becoming an expert driver brings new levels of enjoyment, purpose and safety to your everyday driving. You can neither expect to be satisfied nor bored because the art of expert driving is a continuous learning process. Your increasing self-awareness can never stand idle because working with it is what defines an expert driver.

Gradually blend the extra skills this book expounds into a flowing driving technique with a sensitive, smooth, confident touch.

Stay Safe and Secure

Driving Plans are specific and aim to achieve safer and more accomplished results. They put in process accurate, logically ordered consideration of everything relevant as you drive. What they are *not*, however, is intended as a rigid, formulaic approach that stifles quick reactions to unforeseeable changes of circumstances on the road. Safety – and, therefore, the ability to revise a plan rapidly – must reign supreme.

Driving Plans in Practice

Here are some pictorial Driving Plans to examine:

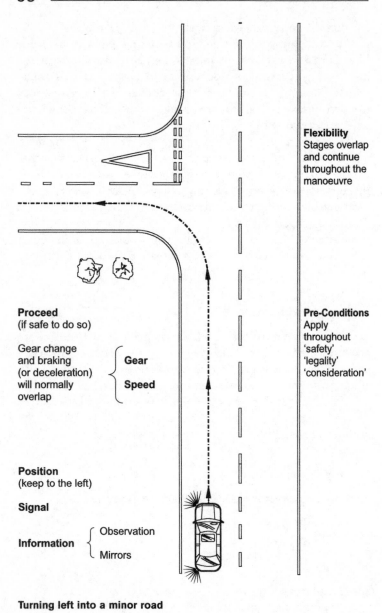

Flexibility
Stages overlap
and continue
throughout the
manoeuvre

Pre-Conditions
Apply
throughout
'safety'
'legality'
'consideration'

Proceed
(if safe to do so)

Gear change
and braking
(or deceleration)　　**Gear**
will normally
overlap　　　　　　**Speed**

Position
(keep to the left)

Signal

Information　{ Observation

　　　　　　　　Mirrors

Turning left into a minor road

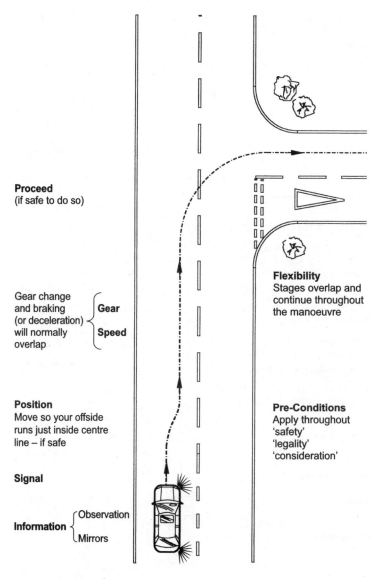

Proceed
(if safe to do so)

Gear change
and braking
(or deceleration)
will normally
overlap
{ **Gear**

Speed

Flexibility
Stages overlap and
continue throughout
the manoeuvre

Position
Move so your offside
runs just inside centre
line – if safe

Pre-Conditions
Apply throughout
'safety'
'legality'
'consideration'

Signal

Information { Observation

Mirrors

Turning right into a minor road

Journey Planning

Every short trip needs some consideration even if it is just to fill up with fuel. (Plan that one by checking you have enough fuel to get to the filling station.) Longer journeys need planning in respect of the best route, the weather, any known road works, stops for rest and refreshment, and possibly, what you need to take with you to keep the children amused!

It is also worth planning for breakdowns. If you are forgetful by nature, carry a proper small container of spare fuel. Membership of one of the motoring organisations is a good idea for most of us but remember they will not carry spares for all cars, so carry some of the more common ones with you, such as bulbs and a fan belt. Also make sure you know how to work your wheel brace and check that your spare wheel is still inflated to the correct pressure. Carry a reflective triangle, a torch and, in winter, at least have a plastic 'scraper' for windscreen ice, and a blanket in case you have to wait to be rescued. In remote areas with snow likely, a spade and snow chains may be essential. A charging cable for your mobile phone is also a good idea – there is nothing worse than needing to make a phone call when your phone battery goes flat!

It is amazing how few people carry a map or, if they do, never look at it. Peter still cannot believe the driver who asked a police patrol officer on the M25 how far it was to the end of the motorway – if the fellow had not found the stationary patrol car, he would probably still be circulating now!

Chapter 5:

Skill Development

If you are already an experienced driver, your driving skills should be at a reasonable level of competence. To become an expert driver these skills will have to be honed and developed to a much higher level. Some skills will have to be taken apart, re-examined and, on occasions, re-learned. They will then have to be put back together again to ensure that your understanding and mastery of those skills and techniques is up to 'expert' level. Specific skills will have to be developed more than others. For example, it is expected that you can brake and change gear successfully but, to develop all the skills necessary to negotiate a series of bends in a smooth and balanced manner will take practice and understanding. As you add one skill to another, it will bring into play many other elements that have to be perfected before you master the overall skill of driving expertly in all situations.

Feedback

To develop your skills to a higher level, it is essential that you practise the self-assessment techniques of Chapter 2, so that you become totally aware of what is happening to the car as it responds to your actions at the controls. Such awareness enables you to make the most of the feedback you receive from the car. This feedback is received through four of your five senses. Let's check over those you should be using whilst driving:

Touch and Body Sensations

You use your hands, feet and body as sensors through which you gather much vital information. You need to be aware of this feedback if you are to develop 'feel' for a car, whether it is on a road, circuit or a loose gravel, rally stage. You need continuously to gather the information the car is sending you and interpret it accurately. For example, if your car starts to lose grip, the quicker you sense and interpret this, the quicker you can correct it.

The steering wheel feedback will tell you a lot about the road surface and the adhesion of the tyres. To an expert driver, the feeling through the steering wheel can also indicate if the tyre pressures are uneven, too soft or too hard. It can even indicate whether the steering geometry is correctly aligned, whether the wheels are balanced or whether the steering joints are worn. If the steering wheel starts to vibrate at a certain speed, it is usually a wheel balance problem. If the car starts to steer itself one way or to slew about when you are not braking, it is usually a tyre with low pressure. Worn joints make your steering increasingly less precise in response.

Likewise the brake pedal can reveal information about the brakes. Some of these indications will be felt through the hands, the feet and the seat at the same time. You can interpret the combined feelings to make a correct diagnosis. For example, if your car slews to one side only when the brakes are applied, you should suspect a brake defect on the other side of the car. If the brake pedal feels spongy, you would immediately suspect that there are air bubbles in the hydraulic system.

Hearing

There is much information to be gathered from listening to your car, particularly the engine. However, many of us tend to block out this aid, with the radio or recorded music. Though this may be a useful way of relaxing on a long journey, there is a great advantage in occasionally turning the radio off and receiving aural feedback from your car by listening to its mechanical sounds. This practice is particularly useful when seeking to enhance your driving skills. For example, to perfect your gear changing, properly matching engine revs to road speed, the best way is by reference to the engine note. Try to think of the sound of the engine as music and become adept at using this harmonious link between you and the car.

Hearing is often what gives you the first inkling of a need to react; for example, when another driver hoots to warn of his presence, or when you hear an emergency siren in the distance or a screech of brakes close at hand.

Another circumstance where hearing will help you is in freezing weather. Then the shift from wet (or a gritted/salted wet combination) to ice may only be detectable by ear. The hiss of water thrown up by your wheels suddenly switches to deathly silence. When negotiating tricky junctions in foggy conditions open your windows. Using sound in such circumstances may be your saviour!

Smell

Your sense of smell can help when you drive. A boiling radiator, hot engine oil on an exhaust pipe, brake fluid on a hot brake, an electrical fire, a burning clutch and tyre smoke each have their distinctive smells as do exhaust fumes infiltrating the passenger compartment. Noticing such early warnings of a problem can save a great deal of money and prevent accidents.

Sight

Eyesight is the predominant sense used in driving. Therefore, if your vision needs correction in order to see properly, then you must wear this whenever you drive (see Chapter 3). However, as we have written earlier, a lot of people who can see well, simply do not see enough! Some people look but do not see; others look at the wrong things, ranging from their passengers' eyes to the scenery at the roadside. Some people see well but interpret what they see poorly. It must also be said that there are a few who hardly seem to look at all.

What is important in the visual context is the ability to scan automatically over the road ahead and to take in other vehicles, people and general things happening in the vicinity, other indicators that may be some distance from the road, and your mirrors and instruments as well. The most common faults are failing to scan far enough ahead and not using peripheral vision.

A very real danger is the effect tiredness has on vision. You may be looking but, if you are too tired, the information may not be being absorbed. It is time to stop and rest. If you do not use all these four of your senses, you cannot be fully aware. If you are not fully aware, your skill levels cannot be fully developed. To become an expert, you must use them all in full measure in order to obtain all the information available and then utilise it in your driving.

Choosing the Right Skill at the Right Time

If you look at other books on driving they tend to be quite dogmatic on which skills to use and when. Some of these skills have not been modified or added to for decades and remain 'cast in stone'.

An example of this dogma is the traditional approach to steering. The pull-push method is the 'accepted' way to steer a car and is taught to learner drivers, as it still is by the police, and even by advanced driving organisations. Have you ever watched a learner trying to manoeuvre in a tight space and seen how difficult the pull-push method makes it to control the car? Why do so many drivers ditch the pull-push method when they have passed their practical driving test? Simple – it is an unnatural way to steer!

If you have ever driven on a skid-pan or in a skid car, you will know how difficult it is to control a rear-wheel skid by using the pull-push method. It is just not quick enough. We have seen advanced police drivers struggling with the skid car because they would not relax and adapt their steering skills to match the reflex quickness required. Fortunately, after much lobbying, we managed to get the police textbook 'Roadcraft' altered at its last rewrite and 'rotational steering' is also now acceptable. However, the dogma lives on and crossing the hands on the steering wheel is still frowned upon by many organisations except, sometimes, in reversing. We, instead, advocate choosing among any of three good ways, selecting the one that is appropriate at the time and which gives you the highest level of safety and control. We return to detail these later in this chapter.

If you wish to become an expert driver, you need to adopt a flexible approach to skills, understand them, try them all out, practise them, adapt them for yourself and have them all in your armoury to be used when needed.

Build on the skills that you have and keep an open mind for new ones presented to you. Do not live in a world of old fashioned techniques – see what works for you and utilise those that increase your safety, enjoyment and overall control. Tune your thinking to work out fresh techniques of your own that match the thrust of this book.

Here are some ideas to get you in training:

Overtaking

Overtaking is not generally taught as a skill when you learn to drive. You are left to learn from experience once you have passed your practical driving test. Yet overtaking is a 'life skill' and should never be thought of as anything else. You do not get too many chances to get it badly wrong!

Planning an overtake provides a good illustration of how the various parts of your Driving Plans (see Chapter 4) need to overlap and be interpreted according to the conditions prevailing.

Pre-Conditions

As with all driving manoeuvres, three essential pre-conditions must apply throughout:

At all times, you must consider whether your overtaking manoeuvre is safe. Will it endanger other road users or yourself? The most important safety aspect is whether you can pass and return to your lane in the distance you have available – if not, you wait until you can.

The manoeuvre must be legal. If you are going to cross double white lines that are against you then you cannot proceed. Similarly, if you have to exceed the speed limit in order to pass in the distance available then you must wait.

You must apply consideration. Do not cut in sharply on the vehicle you are overtaking or cause approaching motorists to brake. If either is in prospect, then the manoeuvre is not on!

Information

Whilst making your Driving Plan for overtaking, you must also consider the following factors:

Scan and be aware of what is happening ahead, behind, and all around you. If a vehicle behind also looks to be considering an overtake, for instance, you will need to give an early right-hand indicator to make it clear that you intend to pull out.

Consider whether you have sufficient space to complete your overtake, and if you have the correct gear to give you the performance needed to pass the vehicle you are overtaking.

Consider the potential for oncoming vehicles to become involved or get 'caught out' by your manoeuvre.

You must be able to get back safely into the nearside without interfering with oncoming traffic, and this largely depends on your judgment of closing speeds and distances in the circumstances. No one should ever have to swerve or slow because of you.

Always ensure that, up to the point of commitment, you can pull back in if necessary.

Do always take into account what is happening behind.

Remember that, once you decide to proceed with the overtake, correct consideration of the above information is going to count and your life may depend on it.

We have tried above to show the range of information about which you must satisfy yourself but every individual pass is also likely to have something special to consider – for example, wet road conditions, poor visibility, low sun, etc.

Signal

The main signal to consider is your righthand indicator well before you pull out. This informs following vehicles as well as distant, approaching traffic. However, much of your intention will also be indicated by your positioning (see below).

Position

There are two aspects to consider with regard to positioning prior to proceeding with your overtake:

1. Vision enhancing adjustments to improve your information gathering, and
2. What your position is 'signalling' to other road users.

Remember that, while moving over to the left may gain you a glimpse up the nearside of the vehicle in front, it may lead a driver behind wrongly to assume that you are not intending to overtake. Therefore you need to watch carefully in your mirrors and give appropriate signals to prevent confusion for others. Your final change in position will be to pull out in order to confirm that it is safe to commit to the overtaking manoeuvre. It is just prior to this outward move that, depending on how long you may have also been continuously monitoring what is behind you, a rapid glance across your right shoulder through the window of your [driver's or rear passenger's] door, can save you from barging into someone already overtaking you, particularly motorcyclists!

Speed

Use throttle control and the brakes, if necessary, to maintain an optimum safe distance behind the vehicle you are planning to overtake. Too close, you not only risk running into the rear of the vehicle should it brake suddenly but also you reduce your view past either side of the vehicle. If you slow and drop back too far, you will have too much ground to make up before you even begin to pass the vehicle. Furthermore, you run the risk of inviting following vehicles to overtake you and slot into the gap you have created in front. It follows that managing vehicle space in this context means just that: managing it.

Gear

Engage a gear ratio (even if driving an automatic) which will allow you to gain a considerable power boost when applying acceleration. If possible your gear selection should also allow you fully to complete your overtake without the need to change gear again until you are past the vehicle being over-taken. Change down well before a prospective 'go' situation so that you are ready to accelerate and then pass the vehicle as quickly as possible.

Proceed (if safe to do so)

You need to confirm that you have a 'go' situation prior to applying power and commencing the overtake. In order to do this you will need to pull out cautiously (if you have not already done so) to obtain the necessary view, before fully committing to the overtake. Remember first the over-your-right-shoulder glance if necessary. If the essential pre-conditions are no longer satisfied, you will need to pull back and continue scanning and planning.

If it is safe to commit, then pass the other vehicle as swiftly as possible and return to the nearside without cutting in.

If, at any stage in passing the vehicle, it were somehow to become apparent that you could not now complete your over-take safely, then it follows that you must, instead, be in a position to drop back in behind. This highlights the need to continue to be aware of what is going on behind you. If

Acknowledge – wave of hand if driver helped you

When clear pull back in

Monitor position of vehicle you are passing

Flexibility
Stages overlap and some continue throughout the manoeuvre

Proceed (if safe to do so)	– 'go' situation steer accelerate

Position – move out to confirm 'go' situation before applying further power

Signal – righthand indicator

Gear – select lower gear early

Speed – maintain distance behind

Position – move out slightly if this increases forward vision but only if safe to do so

Pre-Conditions
Apply throughout
'safety'
'legality'
'consideration'

Information { observation and mirrors throughout

Planning an overtaking manoeuvre

someone is likely, or starts, to close into your gap as you move out, then you must extend the time and distance that you will need to know the road is going to be clear ahead, prior to fully committing yourself.

Acknowledge

A friendly wave of the hand to the person you have overtaken is a good way to encourage courtesy on the road, if the driver helped you.

Flexibility

Remember that, when overtaking, your Driving Plan should be applied in a flexible manner. Observation and planning is a continuous process so, if the situation changes and the essential pre-conditions are no longer satisfactory, you must not proceed. Around the next bend the road may be clear and your early planning could well allow you to overtake efficiently and safely. It is worth remembering that after every bend, or series thereof, there is a straight section of road.

At all times to apply the utmost skill, in attention to potential danger, in judgment of speed and distance, and in recognising the effect your actions may have on others, needs a supreme level of concentration, application, and patience. The greatest possible care needs to be taken to ensure that you pass the other vehicle with total safety.

As congestion on our roads increases daily, we all must accept that opportunities to overtake become fewer. Never risk your life or that of others just to move ahead. If it is not safe then it is not safe! Take care and constantly remain aware of all the dangers of overtaking on today's busy roads. Life is precious – stay safe.

Fast Driving

In today's society and on our overcrowded roads, driving very quickly on public roads is becoming rather more irresponsible and unacceptable. It is not just a question of losing your licence or ending up with a bucket-full of endorsements, or even of ending up in prison. It is a question of having regard for safety and the lives of others as well as your own. An expert driver knows that you do not have to drive absurdly fast in order to enjoy your driving.

Driving at high speed and using a powerful car so as fully to exploit its potential will always be a challenge. Driving on racing circuits, training areas and proving grounds provides the only opportunity where you can do this with relative safety and legality. They are also the places where you can practise and hone more technical driving skills. We would advise that if you really want to drive extremely quickly, then you join a club that offers circuit driving – a 'track driving club'. However, great care still needs to be taken that you do not get carried away when driving on that circuit. You need to be fully aware that road cars are designed for just that and, therefore, have compromises in their chassis design, brakes, tyres and suspension set-ups when compared with fully pre-pared racing cars. Taking road cars onto a circuit needs experienced guidance to keep you safe and enable you to develop the necessary skills and techniques. See Appendix for more information.

Steering

The steering systems fitted to modern cars are precise and require little effort from the driver. However, to operate your steering correctly you must have your seat correctly positioned. Also, your seat belt needs to be adjusted for comfort and so that it does not impede your movements. Sit comfortably upright in your seat, be relaxed at the controls and hold the steering wheel firmly but lightly.

Whilst driving straight ahead, adopt the '10 to 2' or 'quarter to 3' hands' position. Choose whichever suits you and provides the best 'base' from which to turn the wheel.

There are three main methods of steering: rotational, pull-push and fixed-input, all of which an expert driver will use and/or combine as appropriate.

Rotational steering (opposite) is mainly used in slow speed manoeuvring to apply and remove large amounts of steering lock quickly. The hands pass over the 12 o'clock position and cross each other freely in order to enable a lot of steering to be applied efficiently.

Pull-push steering (page 74) is used for general driving. Your hands alternatively pull down one side and push up the other to effect the desired movement of the steering wheel.

Whichever way you wish to turn, you should always pull the wheel down first. This is easier than first pushing it up and offers greater control and stability of the car, especially if you happen to hit a large hole or stone on the road surface.

If you need a larger amount of steering, you must move your hand further up the wheel before pulling down. The more steering you require, the further up the wheel you need to move your hand initially. Indeed, you may need to start at the 12 o'clock position, or beyond, if a lot of steering is going to be needed.

Fixed-input steering is a skill that has been taken from racing drivers. It is largely used when travelling at speed on open roads and involves keeping the hands in a fixed position on the steering wheel. The hands and wheel turn in unison and give better control at speed and more feedback. This skill is explained in more detail in Chapter 8.

The golden rule with steering is not to be constrained by dogma; do what is right for you in the circumstances. There is no reason why your hands should not pass over the 12 o'clock position if that is what you find suitable for yourself in certain conditions. In order to develop your steering skills, you need to be aware of the effectiveness and convenience of methods you choose from time to time. Ask yourself what you noticed most about your technique in any particular prevailing circumstances.

To turn left, start turning the wheel to the left with both hands positioned as they would normally be

Remove your left hand as your right continues turning the wheel

Bring your left hand to the top of the wheel to continue turning it as you remove your right hand

Your right hand returns to pull down from the top of the wheel as your left finishes its pulling down

Continue for more steering or reverse this process to straighten the steering or to turn quickly in the opposite direction

Rotational steering

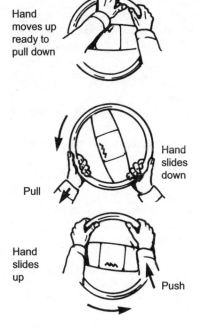

Hand
moves up
ready to
pull down

To turn left, slide your left
hand up to the top of the
wheel and past the 12 o'clock
position if you need to turn a
lot

Pull

Hand
slides
down

Pull the wheel down with your
left hand and, at the same
time, slide your right hand
down ready to push the wheel
up to continue the rotation

Hand
slides
up

Push

Push the wheel up with your
right hand whilst sliding your
left up ready to pull down
again

You can either repeat the
process to get more steering
or reverse it to straighten the
steering or steer to the right

Pull-push steering

Throttle Control

The use of the throttle is a skill often taken for granted by
drivers. Vehicles perform differently when under acceleration
or deceleration and also according to the degree of acceleration
or deceleration. An expert driver will use the throttle to balance
the car by applying the correct amount of power or engine
braking appropriate to the manoeuvre the car is performing.

Everyone has experienced the jarring effect of a novice driver applying the brakes hard and then hitting the accelerator sharply. Much less braking is used by an expert driver because his observation and planning allows earlier decisions to be made – so that speed can mostly be reduced simply by easing the throttle early. This is not only more comfortable than heavy, last-minute braking but also far safer because of the greater stability of the car.

Good observation and planning also removes the need for 'comfort braking' which is seen so often in everyday motoring.

An expert driver is able to drive for long distances with little or no braking. Speed control being largely a matter of early observation and planning, linked with well-disciplined throttle control.

Throttle control will be greatly improved once you become more aware of the effect your application of the accelerator pedal is having on your car. Use it in a measured way that smooths out jerks, enhances the balance of the car, and minimises the need for braking.

Lane Discipline

Always drive in the middle of your lane except when you are positioning for view and/or for added safety margin, or to allow extra room for other vehicles.

Changing lanes is a driving manoeuvre and you must, therefore, first appraise the three pre-conditions: safety, legality and consideration of your effect on other road users. Never change lanes if it is going to inconvenience other drivers. The greatest safety consideration involves traffic approaching from behind, so it is essential that you use all your mirrors and not just the interior mirror, to obtain a full view to the rear. A blind spot check as further described in the next paragraph is also imperative. You must not change lanes if it is illegal to do so, for example, crossing a double-white-line system where the solid line is nearest to you.

Changing lanes requires observation and planning and must include eliminating the rear view 'blind spots' to your right or left, as necessary. If there is following traffic, you will need to give a signal for at least 2 to 3 seconds before changing lanes, and then do so only after completing a quick 'lifesaver', direct look over your shoulder that side to make sure the lane you are moving into is clear of traffic. Remember that, when doing a lifesaver, you have to take your eyes off the road scene ahead, so restrict the glance over your shoulder to a safe moment and duration.

In slow-moving and queuing traffic, be particularly aware of motorcyclists and cyclists coming up between the lanes. You must check and re-check before making any lateral movement to change lanes. Think of the old carpenters' saying – 'measure twice; cut once', which can be paraphrased here as – 'check and double-check, before you manoeuvre'.

Use of Speed

The 21st century motor car gives you the capability of travelling at high speed. The 100+ mph capability most cars have must be managed with wisdom, restraint, legality and consideration for other road users, and so as to secure safety whatever the prevailing conditions. Excess speed not only increases the risk of accidents but also their severity.

You need to develop a 'sense of speed' for every circumstance. Unfortunately, the car insulates its driver from the effects of speed and it is easy to forget just how fast you are travelling. Anyone who has broken down on a motorway will know how intimidating the speed of the general traffic appears even when you are standing well behind the hard shoulder and the barrier if there is one.

To develop a sense of speed, you need to become more generally aware of how fast your car is travelling in relation to its immediate surroundings at any given moment and to think whether this speed is appropriate in the circumstances. It is easy to get into the habit of comparing your speed only with other traffic and thereby to get a false impression. If, instead, you make a point of judging how fast you are travelling in comparison with stationary or slow moving road users, then your impression of speed will change. On a motorway you tend to compare your speed with traffic going in the same direction and at much the same speed. Little wonder that, even going at the legal limit, this does not seem very fast and there is seldom much impression of danger. Standing well behind the barrier at the side of a motorway, however, gives you a totally different appreciation of the speed of the traffic and the feeling of danger.

Motorcyclists tend to have a better sense of speed. On a motorcycle the rider is more exposed to the elements and accordingly has a greater awareness of the effects of speed. What appears slow in a car will feel fast on a motorcycle. Unfortunately, this feeling can give the adrenalin rush sought by a few riders, which leads to a desire for more and more speed and the inevitable risk of a high-speed accident. Fortunately, the majority of motorcyclists use their sense of speed to their advantage and stay safe.

Safety is the paramount objective and an expert driver will always be travelling at an appropriate speed. *Accidents tend to occur when drivers' speeds go beyond their driving and mental capabilities, not when they stay within them.*

You must consider other road users and that includes pedestrians. You need to keep to speed limits. In built-up, 30 mph areas, the commonly risked 40 mph seriously reduces the time a pedestrian has to react to your presence on the road, just as it does your stopping ability, should he step out of turn.

Remember that a speed limit denotes a maximum speed and there will be times when it is not safe to travel at that speed. For example, in very heavy traffic or where there are a lot of children coming out of school, you may have to travel well below the speed limit; at times crawling speed may be too much!

High safety is better than high speed – these two elements do not always go hand-in-hand!

Motorways

In order to deal with the sustained higher speeds on motorways, you need to give yourself many times the space and to plan far earlier before executing a manoeuvre. Sadly, some people do the opposite and drive too close to the vehicle in front and make last-second manoeuvres, often without thought for their mirrors or a signal, or even paying attention to their own peripheral vision.

You must keep your vehicle spacing to a safe distance (the Highway Code rules on Stopping Distances lay down that, in good conditions, you maintain a minimum two-second time gap between you and the vehicle in front; that you double this in wet weather and can need to extend it to ten times in ice and snow). In heavy, fast traffic, forget those figures. You need twice those amounts of spacing at least – in particular, whenever bunching is beginning or happening.

Early planning is essential because, at motorway speeds, a lot can happen in a very short space of time. Look at least a mile ahead or as far as the next curve if that is less; keep your eyes moving to take in all points in between. Never stare at the bumper of the car in front of you.

Know how the signs are used on a motorway, or you will find yourself unable to interpret vital ones quickly enough. If you are planning to leave a motorway, remember that the first sign is one mile from the exit road and the second is half a mile. Watching carefully behind, signal and move when safe into the nearside lane early, so that doing so will not interfere with or frighten anyone already using it or whose path you must cross. Next, look ahead for the slightest evidence that the exit slip road could become blocked. (You may need to prepare for coming to a stop, still in the nearside lane, using your hazard warning lights from the moment of slowing down until it is clear those behind have spotted the danger too.) Give a left signal for leaving the motorway at the latest by the 300-yard countdown marker – or earlier if still travelling fast.

Unless the exit slip will be foreshortened by blockage or excess traffic, use the exit slip to lose speed progressively and smoothly, rather than the nearside lane of the motorway. Try not to slow below the speed of ongoing nearside lane traffic, before you leave it, unless you have to, because, simply, that is inconsiderate driving. Move fully onto the slip road immediately from its start; never dither half on, half off, the motorway.

When joining a motorway, signal right and judge your use of the slip road to accelerate to the speed of the traffic already established on the nearside lane of the motorway – and make sure it is clear by using your mirrors and doing a 'lifesaver' over-your-right-shoulder look, in sufficient time, before blending into the traffic flow.

You will be aware this isn't always as easy as written above! The vital thing is to have an escape plan which vetoes barging in to get on the nearside motorway lane. This is why your 'lifesaver' glance must be well-timed, leaving you the safety of some slip road being left to go, on which to adjust your plan or even come to a stop if you have to. In drastic emergency only, you might have to make that stop on the hard shoulder beyond the slip road end. Better that than run any risk of alarming motorway traffic passing by, never mind causing them to take evasive action.

If you ever do find yourself 'pinned' and having to stop near the end of the slip road, then the thing to do subsequently is to make use of the hard shoulder for picking up to a safe merging speed onto the nearside motorway lane.

Once on the motorway, use the nearside lane for a while to acclimatise to the speed and flow of the traffic there before moving further out for overtaking. Be especially wary, as you merge in, that the motorway traffic itself doesn't just slam to a halt. The first time this happens to you, we hope you will be thankful for having read our book and been warned!

Once you are on the motorway you cannot stop to refer to a map. If you observe and plan correctly you will not have any problems (see Chapter 2, page 26) but, if you do make a mistake, you must leave the motorway at the next exit in order to stop and get directions.

Lane discipline (that is to say according to the correct rules laid down by the Highway Code) is almost a forgotten art on the motorway. Nonetheless, the expert driver still maintains it correctly, ever mindful of all the specific advice given above. Drive in the most lefthand lane unless prevented by traffic density or specific circumstances. After overtaking and unless there is more traffic to pass, your principle must therefore be to return to the nearside lane as soon as it is safe to do so. Never undertake (i.e. pass on the inside) unless in slow-moving, traffic queues. Obviously, common sense is required when changing lanes in busy traffic. But, if done correctly, whether moving out or in, it should not be dangerous. You need to check your mirrors and indicate for at least two seconds (at least four 'clicks') before any such manoeuvre, and then move only if co-operation has been granted by other road users. Your final check must always be your 'lifesaver' look over the appropriate shoulder, lest any driver in a lane *beyond* the one into which you hope to move is about to pull into the same slot.

Before any long motorway journey, make sure both you and the car are fit for the journey. Check your vehicle before setting off and, in particular, the tyre pressures and fluid levels. Don't go on if you become too tired. More than two hours without any rest puts you and others at unnecessary risk.

In the event of breakdown or other emergency, pull over to the hard shoulder as soon as possible and move over to the left of it as far as you can to keep away from the traffic. Try to stop near an emergency phone if circumstances allow. The hard shoulder is one of the most dangerous places to be on the motorway – which is why the Highway Code gives copious advice on this. Do read it *before* you may ever need it!

Try to use the emergency phone if possible, not a mobile, as your picking up of the emergency phone immediately gives the police your exact location. Wait near your vehicle but well away from the carriageway, and preferably well behind the barrier or edge at the back of the hard shoulder.

If you cannot reach the hard shoulder with your vehicle, switch on your hazard lights and exit the car only if/when you can do so safely. If in doubt, everyone should stay in the car with their seat belts on. Do *not* attempt to place a warning sign on the carriageway. If you have a mobile phone, call for assistance.

Finally, only use cruise control when motorway traffic is light. It is rarely appropriate in thick motorway traffic. You find yourself having to brake – cancelling it – and then reset it tediously often. Using it can tempt you to linger with too small a margin of speed whilst you overhaul traffic you are passing, thereby causing frustration behind you.

Gear Changing

Synchromesh has made changing gear a simple, straightforward process. That being said, your timing in relation to speed, loading, gradient and vehicle characteristics, and your skills with accelerator and clutch still demand some finesse to ensure smoothness. These skills are achieved through practice and by feeling what happens each time you change gear. For example, did changing up too early cause the engine to labour? Or down too early make the engine scream? If your engine has a turbo, did you maintain enough revs to maintain turbo assistance? At the precise point of engagement of the new gear (during your clutch pedal release) were the engine revs well matched to your speed in the new gear? Being aware of such feedback by experimenting is the way to learn what is right in various circumstances. Many drivers seem to be quite happy to tolerate rough changes and remain blissfully unaware of how pleasant it can be to execute smooth ones expertly.

Which gear to engage, and when, comes with experience in relation to what you are doing at a particular time. For example, if you wish to travel quickly down a long winding road, you will use the lower gears more often than if you are gently touring along. Returning up the same road will give you the opportunity to experiment with different gear selections. The main thing is to challenge your decisions retrospectively: was the change appropriate? Should it have come earlier or later? Was it to the right gear, or indeed, was the change needed at all?

Automatic gearboxes take a lot of the effort and decision-making out of gear changing. However, you can usually hold lower gears when required, as for negotiating a steep hill or to obtain maximum acceleration from low speed. Changing up or down automatically or manually normally entails a slight lag and/or jerk, but this can be virtually eliminated by subtle use of the throttle. Again, this skill is developed by listening, 'feel', experiment, and learning what's right via feedback.

Cornering

Cornering is a manoeuvre that requires a lot of skill and judgment. Very few drivers have ever been 'taught' cornering and, as a result, it is often done incorrectly. With proper instruction your cornering skills can quickly be improved.

Cornering demands a Driving Plan:

Pre-Conditions

Whilst forming and/or revising your specific Driving Plan, safety, legality and consideration of your effect on other road users must permeate your thinking throughout.

Here is what you should do when you see a bend in the distance. As a development aid, do not be afraid to talk out loud as you build detail into your Plan and its execution, even if only speaking to yourself.

Information

Check all your mirrors and know exactly what is happening around you. At this early stage, endeavour to obtain long, middle distance, and cross views upon which to gauge your Plan. Look into and beyond the bend and try to gain advance views across towards its exit point. You need to look at the severity of the bend, the degree and direction of the camber of the road, traffic in front and behind, the condition of the road surface and the amount of visibility around the bend.

Signal

If you do not need to brake for the bend, traffic may close in behind as you decelerate – if so, you ought to consider pressing your brake pedal just enough to bring on your brake lights and thus alert them that you are slowing down.

Position

Positioning for view was discussed in Chapter 3, page 39. The technique can yield further benefits: for example, you can sometimes 'straighten' a bend if it is legal and safe to do so and this, built in with a well-adjusted entry line, will reduce the severity of the curve. If there is a lot of opposing traffic on a narrow twisty road, you may have little scope to do much. However, on an empty, wide, sweeping bend you may be able to increase your view ahead considerably, as well as straightening it out, provided no one close in your mirrors who might attempt to pass (e.g. a motorcyclist) rules this out.

The fastest route through a corner is not hard to discover if you follow motor racing but racing drivers, remember, do not have to worry about traffic coming the other way. This is seldom the case on the open road and transgressing the centre line – whether marked or absent – even if only to improve your view can be very disconcerting and potentially dangerous to others if overdone. Besides, safety margins are often ignored by those drivers coming towards you, and if you do not allow any room for their mistakes, never mind your own, you will surely hit something before too long.

Having above made clear the overriding necessity of care, it is true that, sometimes, you will come across a deserted section of open road where you can see right across the next bend, the whole of the road surface is clearly visible and unobstructed, and no road marking forbids using all of the road. The decision to 'straighten' such a bend will clearly be yours, but must only be taken in the affirmative after proper observation and planning, and knowing what is happening behind you.

If ever you do plan effectively to cut any corner like this, be very careful that there are no blind spots to your forward vision which could hide an oncoming vehicle, and no blind spots behind that could be concealing trouble, either – and do not forget that prior self-assessment question: 'How might this affect other road users?'; nor afterwards, if appropriate, the question 'Did I cause the remotest stress for anyone else?'

Crossing the centre line is the exception rather than the rule and should only be contemplated on those rare occasions when the view ahead and all-round traffic conditions allow.

Your positioning may need to take account of the condition of the road surface. If the road were partly wet, you would tend to stay on the drier surface even if it was not the best line for the bend. Similarly you might sacrifice the ideal line to avoid travelling on a patch of badly damaged road surface. In neither instance, however, would you let this compromise the safety of others; you would slow down instead.

Speed

The most critical part of cornering is assessing a safe entry speed. As discussed above, you depend on the quality of visual information being gathered on approach, in order to make an informed judgment on this.

In making that judgment, you need, as we have also kept emphasising, to ensure that at every stage you can stop well within the distance you can see to be clear. Therefore, the less view you have into a bend, the slower you must enter it. Your entry speed must match all the vision available, so do early mirror checks and know what is going on all around you.

It is imperative that your entry speed is sufficiently slow. It is far safer to enter a bend too slowly than too quickly. It should be self evident that it is potentially dangerous to enter a bend too quickly and have to brake hard on a curved path. Any misjudgment is made even worse if the road is wet and/or you have opposing traffic.

Just as vital is the gentle re-acceleration, described in Chapter

4, page 55, and below, essential to negotiate the bend itself in a stable well-balanced condition.

Gear

In Chapter 4, page 54, we suggested that braking, if needed before a bend, should come before a gear change down if that is also appropriate. Chapter 8 explains how, with a little extra practice, you can do both at once for a really smooth performance when you are trying to make swift, safe progress. However, as your timing improves with practice, you should, in normal conditions, find yourself less and less having to curb speed by using your brakes. Instead, you aim to make a smooth approach to and round each bend using keenly judged throttle control, linked to good observation and the correct choice of gear being made at the optimum moment.

Proceed

After speed reduction, if necessary, and gear selection where needed but prior to steering for the bend (or it may be for a lesser curve sometimes), make sure your vehicle is balanced and being driven forward under mild acceleration. This sets up the right balance of the forces acting on your car and assists its stability whilst driving round the corner. This delicate throttle balance should be maintained until visibility and road conditions permit (if they do) further controlled acceleration out of the bend.

Acknowledge

It is unlikely you would need to acknowledge anyone whilst cornering. After a series of bends, self-assessment, however, is beneficial: 'What did I notice about my driving?' and 'Did my driving hinder or annoy other road users?' The awareness this process encourages should enable you to continue improving

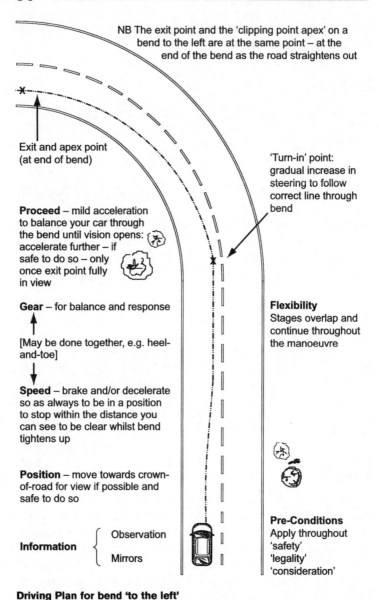

NB The exit point and the 'clipping point apex' on a bend to the left are at the same point – at the end of the bend as the road straightens out

Exit and apex point
(at end of bend)

'Turn-in' point:
gradual increase in
steering to follow
correct line through
bend

Proceed – mild acceleration
to balance your car through
the bend until vision opens:
accelerate further – if
safe to do so – only
once exit point fully
in view

Gear – for balance and response

[May be done together, e.g. heel-
and-toe]

Speed – brake and/or decelerate
so as always to be in a position
to stop within the distance you
can see to be clear whilst bend
tightens up

Position – move towards crown-
of-road for view if possible and
safe to do so

Information { Observation
              { Mirrors

Flexibility
Stages overlap and
continue throughout
the manoeuvre

Pre-Conditions
Apply throughout
'safety'
'legality'
'consideration'

Driving Plan for bend 'to the left'

your cornering skills as well as improving your attitude to driving, all with greater consistency.

Flexibility

Use your Driving Plan with flexibility to help you structure your cornering skills. Follow the order above unless circumstances dictate revised priorities.

Always consider loading when cornering. Your car will feel different when you have passengers or heavy luggage on board and you will have to compensate for this. Take special care with higher vehicles; MPVs and some four-wheel-drive cars have a higher centre of gravity than a normal saloon and this needs to be allowed for when judging cornering speeds.

Once you are steering into a corner, you should not be braking unless it is impossible to avoid doing so. Light and feathered braking can sometimes be achieved but only when the driver has a sufficient level of 'car feel'. Emergency braking on a bend, in case you are ever faced with no alternative, is dealt with further in Chapter 8.

The safest place to practise fast cornering skills is with an instructor on an off-road facility such as a racing track. There you can exploit the handling of a car, hopefully without danger to yourself or others. See Appendix.

Finally – always remember never to accelerate into danger, only away from it!

Safety Margins – How to Create Space

Creating space is another essential aspect of being an expert driver. An 'expert' behind the wheel strives to maintain a zone of safe space around his car at all times. The two main areas of space we are talking about are the one in front and those to the sides of the car.

Less experienced drivers often complain that 'tailgating' is an area of driving that infuriates them. So how do you overcome the problem? The answer is as simple as it is effective –

you just expand the gap in front of you by a slight lift off the throttle. (Do not brake if at all possible.) What this achieves is an added bonus area of space in front of you that you can use to compensate for the lack of space behind. For example, if you anticipate a potential need to brake heavily due to traffic bunching ahead, it creates extra time and space in which to do so without causing drama (emergency braking) by the vehicle behind. In turn, the tailgater benefits from the extra reaction space for any hazard arising.

Controlling safety margins ahead needs to become second nature. Once it is, then no more will you have to 'comfort brake' every time the car in front lifts off the throttle or brakes momentarily for whatever reason. Of course, you may well need to lift from the throttle yourself, but rarely will you have to keep jabbing your brakes on to keep your distance. If you are still doing this, you are probably habitually driving too close to the vehicle in front.

Many drivers appear not to be aware of this essential aspect of safety when trying to 'make progress' through heavy traffic. They seem to think that the closer they are to the vehicle ahead, the faster they will be able to overtake and make 'better' progress – in fact the opposite is true. Creating space ahead allows you more vision of the road ahead. This allows you to plan better and you can always close up when an overtaking opportunity appears.

The need, sometimes, to create space to the sides of your car is likewise often neglected. For example, when driving in a town street, parked cars may make the available space quite limited and the potential for accidents higher. Should someone open a car door into your path or a pedestrian walk from between two parked cars, you will need to take avoiding action. The more space you have, the easier it is to brake or deviate safely.

If sufficient lateral space is not achievable, then you must slow down. Match your speed to the available space on the road. As an expert driver you will make this compensation in your speed but you cannot expect every other driver to do the same. You must be prepared to allow for the oncoming driver who is going far too quickly in tight circumstances. This is done by slowing even more, or indeed stopping if necessary, to let the other driver through.

YOU have to be the person who thinks about creating space and reducing speed where necessary – others may not be thinking or paying attention. Never rely on others to bring safety into the equation – ever!

Responsibility and Risk Assessment

The exercise of restraint and self-control is the paramount safety initiative behind a steering wheel. The less self control you have, the less responsibly you will drive. Being a responsible driver is as important as being a responsible person in society. Some people are happy to accept this and drive accordingly; others, alas, are not and drive dangerously as a result. Although you may act responsibly, you can never assume that another driver will.

Therefore, you must think for others as well as yourself and use your expert ability to ensure a safe outcome.

You must become an expert at correctly assessing risk factors when you are driving. There are two main types of risk on which to focus:

(a)   Potential risk
(b)   Actual risk (a threat to safety).

You want to ensure that, wherever possible, any potential risk cannot escalate into an actual threat to safety on the road. High awareness in your observation and sound contingency planning must travel hand-in-hand. This is a basic element of expert driving.

Let's consider a practical example. Imagine you are travelling along a busy, moderately wide, secondary road following a slow-moving car that you wish to overtake. Behind you is another car that is also being held up by the vehicle in front. Not far ahead is a junction to your right which appears to be clear and, as you pull out slightly for a better look, you can see a cyclist in the far distance on your side of the road.

So far, there has been no indication that the driver in front might want to turn right and it will shortly be too late for him to do that anyway. However, as you plan for this prospective overtake, you need to assess all the potential risks. Firstly, could a vehicle yet emerge from the junction to the right and pull into your path just as you start the overtaking manoeuvre? Secondly, can you pass the vehicle in front before it starts to pull out to pass the cyclist? Thirdly, what is the driver behind likely to do whilst you are planning or carrying through your manoeuvre? Fourthly, is there any traffic coming in the opposite direction and, if there isn't, is there enough clear open road to ensure your overtake would not be affected by traffic coming into view? Finally, is the car you are intending to overtake still being driven steadily and with no signs that the driver might suddenly deviate, brake, accelerate or be frightened by your manoeuvre?

All the above are potential risks that you need to consider in this example. In deciding whether to proceed, you have to decide if any of these risks can develop into an actual threat to safety. If you commit yourself and then a car appears in the junction or your view into the side road remains too restricted so that a car could still be hidden, your safety, as well as that of everyone else, is going to be threatened. Don't do it! Similarly, if you start your overtake at the time that the slower vehicle begins to pull out to pass the cyclist, you are endangering everyone on that section of road. In particular, the cyclist is then very vulnerable. So don't do that either!

Some of the risks can be dealt with by giving a well-timed signal and using appropriate positioning of your car. Although you may have considered and/or seen all the potential risks ahead, remember that the driver following may not have. If you decide not to overtake because of them, it follows that there is always a possibility the driver behind may then decide to have a shot. A dab on the pedal to bring on your brake lights should discourage him, rather than antagonise him. Your positioning, however, remains critical. This is because if you stay towards the crown-of-the-road it should indicate your continuing intention to overtake – if, instead, you pull back towards your nearside, that may even encourage him to try to pass you both, risks unseen.

Always give your righthand indicator when you intend to overtake. It not only informs traffic behind and approaching in the distance but, unless he is 'asleep', also lets the driver you are passing know your intentions. If you are unsure of the intentions of the driver you are about to overtake, then the risk may be too high and, again, you must delay your manoeuvre.

If you sense any danger always hold back and be patient. Driving situations are very fluid and it will not be long before the dangers pass, enabling you to pick up speed and return to planning your overtake in both safety and harmony with other road users.

You have a major part to play in assessing all such risks, so that you can do your best to reduce them for all concerned. To rely exclusively on others being able to see potential risks and react properly is, unfortunately, naïve.

Never take a casual attitude towards pedestrians. Their physical vulnerability is unprotected. Young children and the elderly are at a higher risk: children because of the immediacy with which they can change direction; the elderly because they may only be able to manage slow reactions and movement. You *must* take account of these factors.

Smoothness and Flow

Smoothness has always been the hallmark of an expert driver. The ability to change gear, steer, brake or accelerate with incredible flow, finesse and feel is a joy to behold.

The faster you drive, the smoother you need to become because any slips in technique are naturally magnified at higher speeds. Jerky steering, throttle, or injudicious braking during cornering can certainly trigger loss of control if your speed is close to the limit of adhesion already. Contrast this with an expert whose near seamless steering and measured throttle balances his car with full retention of overall stability.

On exiting a bend, it is important that when you apply more throttle, you do this in conjunction with a smooth and progressive unwinding of your steering angle.

You can only really learn the value of this when driving hard on a circuit or the wide-open spaces of a proving ground. We recommend you take such an opportunity if ever you can. (See Appendix.) On the track, once you have developed a degree of feel for the car, you should be able, quite quickly, to corner at a speed where your car is absolutely on the limit, yet never tips over its limit. But woe betide you if you then make any sudden, jerky movement of the steering, brakes or throttle. That would probably result in a spin or a trip into the gravel!

Being in control of your emotions whilst achieving such a feat is vital. You can enjoy exploring the limits on the circuit or proving ground but must exercise sufficient self-control never to attempt it on the public road. The unpredictable nature of events on public roads rules it out. However, if you can gain such skills off the road, you will certainly be able to improve your car balance and vehicle stability when cornering at lesser speeds on public highways.

Achieving near perfect smoothness demands becoming critically aware of how your inputs to the controls are affecting your car's balance and ride. When you apply the brakes, ask yourself how it affected the smoothness of the car. When you apply steering, ask yourself whether your car remained balanced and stable or was heeling over too much, feeling unsteady and close to its limits. By persevering with asking yourself these types of questions you will soon reach the level of awareness that underpins smoothness.

When an expert driver uses his brakes or throttle, it is always smoothly and progressively. Again, when releasing either, this is also done in a controlled manner. So, if you have not refined this technique before, then next time you need to reduce throttle, try taking a second or two gradually to release the pedal rather than taking your foot straight off it. You will find the difference is remarkable and will be much appreciated by your passengers. Similarly when applying or releasing the brake pedal, take time to apply or release it gradually. Jabbing, jerky or uncontrolled use of your brakes or throttle results in an unstable car and passengers complaining about your poor driving.

Developing a flowing style and fitting in with the road configuration and traffic around him is another focus that the expert keeps totally under control. He invariably arrives at any hazard, turning or whatever, in the right position, in the right gear and at the correct speed. His slick application of the controls to achieve this is hardly noticed by passengers.

In summary always be smooth and gentle. Steer with 'feel', brake with finesse and apply your throttle with delicacy. Take time to brake or accelerate progressively. Operate your controls in one continuous flow wherever you can. Always be aware of the consequences of your actions and use this knowledge constantly to improve your skills.

Chapter 6:

Skills – No. 1 Skidding

Objectives

Expert driving requires you to develop your skill in all its aspects. The term 'driving' is quite broad and includes attitude, knowledge and skills. This and the following two chapters deal more specifically with the skills and techniques that are most essential. They are mainly dedicated to expanding what you already know in order to build a solid foundation for your driving skills and experience.

Not all driving skills can easily or safely be learnt on the road. Experience restricted to roadwork misses much. For example, it is impractical and potentially dangerous to practise skidding techniques on the public road! However, having an open mind, reading widely, and seizing every safe opportunity that may arise, will produce for you many enjoyable and entertaining ways of developing your skills. Driving is driving, whether it is on the road, circuit, rally stage or wet surfaces on a skid-pan or proving ground. Grab such chances where you can. (See Appendix.) All of these help to make a totally rounded driver. Nothing fazes an expert and nothing should stand in the way for you to achieve this type of driving experience.

This chapter covers skidding and how to control a skid. Chapter 7, Skills No. 2 Braking, then takes an in depth look at braking techniques. Chapter 8, Skills No. 3 examines circuit driving which is another area of driving that has huge advantages when mastered, giving you a far better understanding of car handling, road holding, braking etc. Furthermore, rally driving and practice on large open areas, such as an empty runway, have something to offer every driver. They provide a superb way to understand and learn advanced car control techniques.

Although these chapters are mainly skill based your mental approach will still play an important part in developing them and, most importantly, keep you safe whilst learning.

We have no doubt that you will have great fun slipping and sliding around on a skid training session and enjoy enormously perhaps being able to drive very quickly round a race circuit in total harmony with your car. It will extend your 'feel' for a car and this will bring you huge rewards in skill development as well as giving you hours of pleasure. However, always remember, back on the public road, that that road is neither a skid-pan nor racing circuit; nor can it ever be treated so.

Skidding

Have you ever been involved in a skid?
Did you feel in control of the outcome?
Did you panic?
Did you just hit the brakes?

A better understanding of the causes and effects of skidding will lead inevitably to you being able to avoid most skids and to deal effectively with those that do occur. The driver causes nearly all skids. However, most people would blame the road or weather conditions should they ever be involved in a skid – the last person they blame is themselves! Skids are caused, they do not just happen. It is strange how we are always prepared to blame everything else but ourselves when things go wrong.

Some time ago, after a certain driver had skidded on black ice and crashed his car, he blamed the black ice for the skid. When interviewed he said that excessive speed was not the cause but the ice had 'forced' the skid. When asked how fast he was driving in such bad conditions he remarked that he was doing about 15 mph, which he did not consider as excessive. However, would he have skidded if he had been driving at, say, 4 mph? Highly unlikely is the answer. So excessive speed was one cause. The only mitigating factors possibly open to him were to do with whether or not he could have seen the ice or should have been aware of it having regard to the weather conditions.

Skids only take place because a driver makes the car do so and 'inappropriate' speed will invariably be somewhere in the skidding equation. If you develop a correct sense of speed for each and every occasion – speeds that match circumstances with safety – skids will seldom take place and you will rarely be called upon to exercise your skid control skills. Unfortunately, skids do happen no matter how careful you are; for example, other drivers can cause you to brake harshly or swerve sharply and thereby induce a skid. Thus, the more you understand about the causes and control of skids and practise your skills, the more able you will be to avert them and minimise their effects when they do arise.

Smoothness and finesse with your car controls will play a large part in eliminating skids in the first place. Clearly, poor tyres or worn suspension parts can cause skids on slippery surfaces. The main purpose of the suspension system is to allow the tyres to remain in contact with the undulating road surface whilst the car body remains reasonably stable. If the suspension becomes worn, particularly the shock absorbers, the wheels begin to bounce off the bumps in the road, leading to loss of grip. Furthermore, wear in the suspension and steering joints will result in changes to the various preset steering and suspension set-ups causing, for example, changes in the understeer/oversteer characteristics of the car. (These are discussed in the next few pages.) However, with a properly maintained car, skids are mainly due to poor control by the driver. Smoothness has a role to play in all driving but is critically important when driving on surfaces where skidding may occur, such as ice, snow, wet leaves, gravel and surface water.

It is worth mentioning here that front-wheel-drive cars pull their chassis along, whereas rear-wheel-drive cars push their chassis. Of course, four-wheel-drive cars both push and pull the chassis in harmony.

Defining a Skid

Let us start by explaining what a skid is and how skids are caused. We also need to recognise the different types of skid. The control techniques you need to learn, to ensure that safety prevails, can only follow from a proper understanding of this information.

A skid develops when the grip of the tyres is overcome by the forces acting on the vehicle.

In simple terms, something is being done by the driver, to the car – to make the tyres lose their grip on the road. There are many causes of skids but all are related to driver inputs, with the main four being:

- Excessive speed for the prevailing conditions or circumstances
- Hard or inappropriate acceleration
- Sudden or too severe braking
- Heavy-handed or sharp steering

A skid can develop just by doing one of the above, or a combination of two or more. For example, consider a car being driven round a long, slippery bend by an inexperienced driver in a hurry. The accelerator is hard down and, in the attempt to get round, the steering is being applied more and more earnestly as the car begins to drift because of the excessive speed. All it needs is for this driver to panic and land on the brakes as his car teeters on the brink and it will invariably skid and end up in the shrubbery, or worse. All four main causes are present in this one incident!

There are various broad types of skid and each needs to be experienced in order to get the 'feel' of what is happening to the car. *Gaining such experience and developing the control skills with which best to counteract skids demands practice off the road preferably at a proper training facility.* Details of such facilities can normally be obtained from police driving schools or advanced driving organisations.

Understeer and Oversteer

In order to describe skidding, it is first necessary to understand the two terms 'understeer' and 'oversteer'. A variable degree of slip takes place relative to the steered course of the front wheels, known as the 'slip angle'; as a result those wheels follow a slightly wider trajectory than might be expected for the steering lock applied. The effect is that the car does not turn as tightly as the amount you have turned the steering wheel might suggest – in other words, it 'understeers'. In practical terms, the normal, non-skidding slip angle is too small to detect from the driving seat.

The degree of this understeer is dictated by the suspension set-up and how much the tyres deflect during cornering.

As the term indicates, 'oversteer' is, in effect, the direct opposite of understeer. Here the car turns a tighter path than might be expected for the steering lock applied – in other words it 'oversteers'. Generally, oversteer only occurs when the angle being 'slipped' at the rear wheels exceeds both their design tolerance and that of the angle being 'slipped' at the front wheels. In this instance, therefore, the car turns more tightly than suggested by the amount you have turned the steering wheel.

If your front wheels completely lose their grip on a bend then you will have a pronounced understeer effect, as your car will no longer be responding to the steering wheel. This is called an understeer skid and it is at once obvious from behind the wheel. Similarly, if your rear wheels start to skid while cornering and the back of your car slides out, this rapidly leads to your front wheels describing a tighter curve – and so this is called an oversteer skid. Again, you will be aware of it instantly;

however, it often proves less possible to counteract than an understeer skid.

It has become common, though somewhat misleading, practice to call understeer skids and oversteer skids simply by the terms, understeer and oversteer.

Front-Wheel Skids (Understeer)

There are two types of front-wheel, cornering skid. The first is known by the general term for front-wheel skids of this kind, whilst the second refers to a particular type of understeer:

- Understeer
- Power understeer

Understeer occurs when, during a bend, the front wheels partially, or totally, lose their grip on the road. The front wheels control the steering so, as well as the front of the car sliding sideways, the steering effect will be reduced or lost.

In broad terms, a front-wheel skid (understeer) can be felt

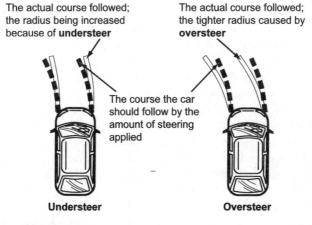

The actual course followed; the radius being increased because of **understeer**

The actual course followed; the tighter radius caused by **oversteer**

The course the car should follow by the amount of steering applied

Understeer   **Oversteer**

Understeer/Oversteer

as the car pushing straight on and away from the steered path round a curve. In other words, because the front wheels are sliding, they are unable to steer the car on the correct path.

It is easy to sense 'understeer'. You must respond as soon and as smoothly as possible.

Where many drivers get things partly wrong in trying to correct a front-wheel skid is that they begin to apply even more steering because the car is heading straight on instead of going round the curve. All this achieves is to prolong the skid.

Off-road practice will modify this incorrect reaction in favour of the right ones explained further below under recovery from understeer.

Front-wheel-drive cars are more likely to develop understeer and power understeer because the drive train is at the front rather than at the back. Clearly, if too much power is applied, your front tyres will lose their grip, causing a front-wheel skid – hence the term 'power understeer'. This condition most often occurs with excessive acceleration going round a bend in the wet; however, it can also occur in dry conditions although it is less pronounced. You feel the car begin to 'plough-on' and, unless you ease off the power and/or reduce your steering lock, this understeer will continue. Normally, only front-wheel-drive and, less so, four-wheel-drive, cars can develop power understeer. However, the condition can be contrived with rear-wheel drive if excessive steering angle is whipped on, though it would probably be a purposeless exercise.

All vehicles, whether front-, rear- or four-wheel-drive, have their chassis characteristics tuned by test drivers and chassis engineers to develop 'initial' understeer when cornering. This in-built safety feature is there because, should the average driver go into a bend too quickly, he would get an early feeling of understeer, even if he did not know what exactly was happening. One natural reaction to such a feeling is to ease off the accelerator which, as you will see next, is the major part of controlling understeer. Provided this 'average' driver knows already that he should not be trying to steer more, his car should then settle down so that he can then complete the bend.

Recovery from a Front-Wheel Skid (Understeer)

Controlling understeer and bringing the car back into line should be very straightforward. You do not have to be an expert and, what is more, the correct control technique is mostly a natural response. All you do is remove the cause. Most often this means simply lifting your foot gently off your accelerator for the necessary moment or two.

With severe understeer, you may also have to remove some of the steering lock being applied. For mild understeer, however, this isn't necessary. Easing off your throttle will be enough for the front wheels to regain their grip and re-establish steering control; you then re-establish a sufficient but lesser level of acceleration as appropriate. Should your reaction with your throttle alone not prove sufficient, then even quite a small reduction in steering angle, gently removed, coupled with your lifting off the power, ought to rectify all but the worst cases of understeer and power understeer.

In essence, whether it is understeer or power understeer, your recovery technique is the same – remove the main cause by easing off your accelerator. However, if your foot reaction is too sudden or overdone, your car will tend to turn more sharply into the corner as grip is re-established and this can further destabilise your progress. Some residual throttle needs to be maintained so as to take your car where you are trying to steer it. So, smoothness, as emphasised earlier, is essential in all aspects of controlling understeer.

We stress again that, in order to learn these recovery techniques, you will have to be off public roads and in an area where the deliberate induction of such skids can bring no harm to you or to anyone else.

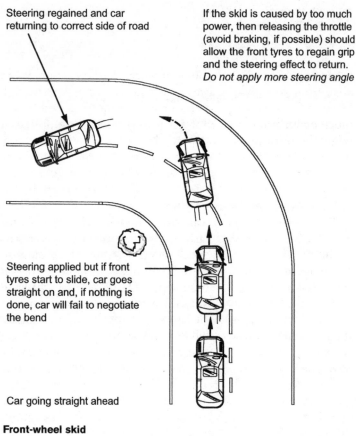

Steering regained and car returning to correct side of road

If the skid is caused by too much power, then releasing the throttle (avoid braking, if possible) should allow the front tyres to regain grip and the steering effect to return. *Do not apply more steering angle*

Steering applied but if front tyres start to slide, car goes straight on and, if nothing is done, car will fail to negotiate the bend

Car going straight ahead

Front-wheel skid

Rear-Wheel Skids (Oversteer)

Rear-wheel skids generally only occur on rear-wheel-drive cars. Because all the power goes to the rear wheels, too much of it for the grip of the rear tyres will make them spin, slide or both.

Overall, there are three main types of rear-wheel skid. The first is the general term and the other two are particular variations:

- Oversteer
- Power oversteer
- Lift-off oversteer

Oversteer happens when your rear wheels lose their grip. It can arise from too much power as explained above, or through lifting off the throttle too sharply in a bend. If caused by too much power being applied to the rear wheels, for example, as it might be during a 'grand prix' start, you know it instantly because the back of your car straightaway snakes out of line and tries to 'overtake' the front. This is called 'power oversteer'. If due to abrupt 'lift-off' of the throttle during cornering, it is called 'lift-off oversteer'.

This lift-off oversteer can occasionally occur with front-wheel drive too, particularly in wet weather. However, the lift-off induced rear-wheel skid is getting less and less common as modern-day chassis are better designed and tuned to stay on course even when you do suddenly lift off your throttle in mid-corner. Eventually, no doubt, traction and safety support systems – covered by our Chapter 9 – will almost eliminate such skids irrespective of what you do wrong.

However, the laws of physics cannot be totally overcome by technology so there will always be the need for you to be able to sort out a skidding problem. Technology may be taking away many demands from you but it will never provide the total solution – we humans will always make mistakes behind the wheel!

Recovery from a Rear-Wheel Skid (Oversteer)

A rear-wheel skid is inherently more difficult to counteract and control and can turn vicious if allowed to get out of hand. To the extent excess power has triggered the skid, for example, as with snaking on a race start, you must first cut that power smoothly back below the problem level. Simultaneously, the main technique you need to apply is called 'opposite lock', 'counter steering', or 'steering into the skid'. You steer in the opposite direction to the way your car was meant to be travelling but in the same direction as the skid. For instance, going round a bend to the left, a rear-wheel skid makes the rear of your car step out to the right and you must steer right before you can regain control. Hence the term 'opposite lock' because you really wish the car to go to the left. Your instant purpose is to prevent the rear of the car pivoting around the front wheels. Opposite lock will straighten the car up and the lefthand lock can then be reapplied as soon as it's possible. This combination of scotching excess power and steering into the skid can normally be very short lived; your immediate, subsequent aim is then to restore just enough power (directly you are able also to apply sufficient steering back to the left) to take you to safety before having left the road, or worse . . . Be warned! This skill needs highly expert car 'feel' and the right balance of forces to recover control – so your learning has to be done safely, and most certainly *off* public roads.

The key to successful remedial steering lies in the correct link with carefully measured throttle control. The skid happens because the grip of the rear tyres cannot hold against the speed and/or power applied at the degree of angle steered on the road surface conditions being encountered at the time. By carefully easing the throttle as well as applying corrective steering, you should be able to get your car to settle down with its ability to take the rest of the bend duly restored.

The control of oversteer, then, is essentially formed around how much opposite lock steering needs to be applied and the use of balanced throttle control. The more your car skids sideways, the more opposite lock you need. The advantage of off-road practice is that you can quickly learn to 'feel' what to do – and without panicking. Without knowing the theory and having some off-road practice, the general reaction to oversteer is to hit the brakes. Doing so at anything more than a very slow speed, you are likely to lose control totally and land up wherever the skid takes its course. Whereas, with some experience under your belt, most such skids can be safely corrected. Nonetheless, we stress again that any deliberate induction of

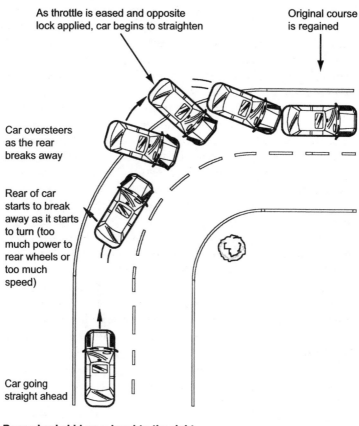

As throttle is eased and opposite lock applied, car begins to straighten

Original course is regained

Car oversteers as the rear breaks away

Rear of car starts to break away as it starts to turn (too much power to rear wheels or too much speed)

Car going straight ahead

Rear-wheel skid on a bend to the right

oversteer is out of order on public roads. These skids are not safe enough for that!

Rally and race drivers actually use power oversteer to steer the car in certain circumstances. They balance power and steering angle to maintain a controlled slide (drift) with their back wheels stepped outward to conform with the line of the corner. Needless to say, this technique takes a lot of practice and is only for off-road conditions.

Although the techniques to control oversteer are more demanding than for understeer, they are surprisingly easy to master with proper, off-road, skid training. A couple of enjoyable sessions on the skid-pan or in a skid car will do the trick. Indeed, in our view, every driver should spend time on a skid facility to learn the rudiments of skid control.

The best way to prevent skids in the first place is not to drive beyond the personal limits of your experience or the physical limits of your car. Always take account of the conditions of the road surface and the weather that prevail. Of course, skids do occur from time to time, and this is why we so heartily recommend that the best form of defence is to attack with some bespoke training sessions. See Appendix to find a venue for these.

If you get the chance to see a rally or stock-car racing driver 'power slide' round a circuit or proving ground, with the rear of his car hanging out – seemingly out of control to the untrained eye – it is a joy to watch. His skill keeping his car at ridiculous angles as he feeds in both sensitive steering and delicate throttle inputs is what will decide whether he wins. He senses what needs to be done from the feedback presented to him by the car, mostly, we would suggest, through his backside. Many years ago a former ace grand prix driver was asked, 'What makes a great race car driver?' He confirmed this in three words – 'A sensitive arse!'

The only thing better than watching such expertise is having a go yourself! However, do remember that it is a racing skill, not a public road one.

Aquaplaning (Through Excess Speed)

Vehicles can only be driven safely in wet conditions because of the tread pattern of their tyres. The tread has the effect of a squeegee and removes the water from between the tyre and the road surface, allowing grip to be maintained. If the tyre has no tread and the road surface drainage is poor then it does not take much rain on the surface before the tyre loses grip. This fact is well illustrated by racing cars with slick tyres, when they are caught out by a heavy shower and begin to slip and slide all over the place. Normally, the race has to be stopped so that treaded, wet-weather tyres can be fitted.

The tread pattern can only cope with a finite amount of water and the more worn the tyre, the less water it can shift. Consequently, if a car is driven at such a high speed that the tread pattern cannot remove all the water, the excess will build up in front of, and subsequently under, the tyre. In any particular wet conditions, there will be a critical uppermost speed at which each tyre ceases to turn and instead starts to plane across the water – hence the term 'aquaplaning'. *This is mighty dangerous because you can no longer steer; nor can you brake effectively without any input from the aquaplaning wheels.*

Tyre size, tread pattern and depth are all relevant to the speed at which aquaplaning takes place, as is the depth of water and the nature of the road surface. Aquaplaning rarely occurs below 40 mph and is more common over 55 mph. However, in extreme circumstances, as with racing cars with totally bald tyres, aquaplaning can occur at quite slow speeds.

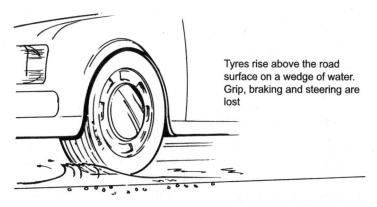

Tyres rise above the road surface on a wedge of water. Grip, braking and steering are lost

If water builds up between the road and the tyre the car will aquaplane

The symptoms of aquaplaning are that the steering will go light and the rear of the vehicle may also start giving the impression of being loose and unstable.

Recovery from Excess Speed Aquaplaning

Use three basic rules to restore control:

1. Lift off your throttle to reduce driven power.
2. Do not turn your steering other than to straighten it.
3. Do not brake.

Look ahead, and allow your car to slow down whilst steering straight ahead with both hands holding the wheel, until the tread pattern can once again cope with all the water. Once it can, you will feel the steering become firmer as you regain control and can again steer where you want to go.

Aquaplaning (Through Braking)

Any sudden sharp braking in very wet conditions can give rise to aquaplaning down to much slower speeds. What happens is that, if you lock your wheels, the tread squeegee mechanism for clearing the water is at once lost. The wheels no longer rolling means huge amounts of water force their way between your stopped tyres and the road – to the point, sometimes, that, instead of skidding still in touch with the road surface, those wheels simply aquaplane on the mini water 'mountains' being created.

Recovery from Braking Aquaplaning

Unless you swiftly release your brakes this planing can then continue down the scale – braking effect *and* steering gone – until the weight of your vehicle can push your tyres back down onto the road. From that point the wheels can still skid, steering still out of action, along the wet surface if you keep your brakes frozen on! So you have to learn to release them enough to let those wheels roll. Then your treads have a chance to disperse the water and the rubber to grip instead of slide.

Four-Wheel Skids (All-Wheel Skid)

A four-wheel skid is, as the name implies, where all four wheels lose their grip on the road simultaneously. In its less severe form, whilst cornering, it is called a four-wheel drift, where the car is gently moving sideways across the road but still managing to go partly round the corner. Four-wheel skids are caused by excessive speed, by locking up all four wheels with the brakes, or by using too much power with a four-wheel-drive car (see below).

Recovery from a Four-Wheel Skid

Recovery from a four-wheel skid is dependent on its cause. If either excessive speed or too much power causes the skid, then you must react with reflex speed but respond gently by lifting off your throttle smoothly, so that your wheels can regain their grip as your car starts to slow. Wherever possible, braking should be avoided but, if necessary, once grip has been regained, you can brake, using great care not simply to exchange your plight for a four-wheel, braking skid.

If your skid has been induced under braking then, again, you need reflex speed but a measured response. You must ease brake pressure enough so that grip can be regained and the wheels start to turn. If more braking is still required, you have to resume this with great sensitivity, to avoid a continuation of the skid. This demands careful technique all explained in more detail in the next chapter.

Four-Wheel-Drive Vehicles

There are two main types of four-wheel-drive vehicles. Some have the facility to run in two-wheel-drive mode until you select four-wheel drive. (Clearly, these react just as would any similar two-wheel-drive vehicle unless/until that selection is made.) The more common ones simply have permanently engaged four-wheel drive. The amount of drive going to each of the four wheels can vary depending on the sophistication of the drive-train mechanism. In some with extra safety systems, for example, the drive will automatically be removed from a wheel that loses grip thus stopping it sliding on the road. A few, very sophisticated systems also have 'yaw' control where the car senses sideways movement and computes how much drive should go to each wheel individually. The speed and sideways angles with which these cars can corner is truly exceptional. Owners of vehicles as sophisticated as this must exercise considerable self-discipline to avoid cornering at speeds from which they cannot stop if something solid lies in their path further round the bend.

As the drive on four-wheel-drive cars is fed through all the wheels, they are prone to having a 'neutral' feel in their handling characteristics; i.e. exhibiting neither a tendency to understeer nor oversteer. Nonetheless, as explained earlier in this chapter, four-wheel-drive cars also have a degree of understeer designed into their chassis for safety purposes when cornering.

Four-wheel-drive cars are less likely to skid in normal driving conditions – it is quite difficult to induce power oversteer or power understeer or a four-wheel, power skid, when the drive is transmitted spread through all four wheels. However, some four-wheel-drive systems are designed to be able to give more drive to one pair of wheels than the other and, in extreme circumstances, power oversteer or understeer can be induced.

Some people feel invincible in four-wheel-drive cars and therefore tend to drive faster in difficult conditions than if they were in a two-wheel-drive vehicle. The limits of adhesion under power are higher and thus the excesses in which the driver can indulge are greater, but beware. You still only have four tyres trying to grip the road. When a four-wheel-drive car exceeds its limitations there is usually serious trouble waiting.

Whilst the limits are higher, so are the consequences if you overstep the mark.

You need to appreciate that the grip of your tyres is only the same as with other forms of drive. The difference is simply that they can cope with more power because it is spread throughout four tyres not two. Test-driving in the wet, ice or snow, on an empty airfield apron or similar wide-open space, should let you explore the limits of adhesion and traction of a four-wheel-drive chassis in comparative safety. It's best for you to have someone experienced beside you to give guidance. A four-wheel drift can be scary and it is at this point that things will go pear-shaped if you decide that braking would be a good idea! However, you should quite quickly grasp the knack of proper control techniques if instructed well.

Furthermore, *four-wheel-drive vehicles do not have any better braking than two-wheel-drive cars.* All cars have brakes on all four wheels and their braking performance is on a par. Therefore, although a four-wheel-drive vehicle may feel more sure-footed in slippery conditions, it is no more able to slow down and stop, than a two-wheel-drive car.

'Panic-Freeze' Syndrome

If you have ever been involved in a scary driving situation you may remember your emotions rising to the point where you felt incapable of staying calm and reacting correctly. For example, you are driving round a bend in slippery conditions when you experience the first rear-wheel skid of your driving career. Instead of applying the correct action to control the skid you freeze and either lock on the brakes or find that you are incapable of doing anything at all. Hopefully, still being a novice, this occurs at slow speed and, apart perhaps from being embarrassed at sliding onto the wrong side of the road, no accident occurs.

The 'panic-freeze' syndrome stops you thinking and react-ing properly but, in an emergency, there is an urgent need to think and act clearly. Overcoming the 'panic-freeze' instinct takes great emotional control and, sometimes, years of practice. Many drivers never get that far. When faced with a critical emergency situation they still automatically tense up. This normal human reaction starves your brain of the ability to respond rationally. You either fail to react altogether or you respond incorrectly, losing the opportunity to use your skills to recover from the situation.

It is in overcoming panic-freeze that drivers who have spent time on a proper skid facility really shine. They have already experienced different types of skid many times and have become schooled into reacting in an appropriate way. Although such moments might be scary, these drivers do not freeze. Both the mind and, hopefully, the skids are controlled, with any danger being averted.

Braking in a Skid

Braking in any skid is to be avoided unless absolutely necessary. It is possible to brake but the sensitivity required is beyond what most people can attain in an emergency.

You might, on reading the above, ask yourself 'What good, anyway, would braking be towards regaining control of a sliding sideways skid?' However, there may be a point – you might want to attempt any braking possible if you wanted to slow down before you crashed!

In normal driving conditions, even on wet or slippery surfaces, you should have little difficulty in judging braking distances. Unfortunately, in an emergency, your skill can sometimes disappear, even with only a modicum of 'panic-freeze' setting in. You apply your brakes too hard, the wheels lock, steering control is lost, and the end result is in the lap of the gods! If you have an ABS (Anti-lock Braking System) it may come to your rescue but, without an ABS, a fair bit more skill may be required and this is one of the subjects of our next chapter.

Further Points on Skidding

As we have said, most cars inherently understeer. The designs of suspension systems and tyres are now so good that the majority of vehicles are very forgiving of mistakes by the driver. Clearly, if you are heavy-footed on power or harsh on braking, any car may skid, but most will quickly settle once the cause is removed. This means that even a driver of average skill levels can correct his mistakes without too much difficulty, always provided he has the know-how.

However, some cars have an 'entertaining' chassis; for example, as noted earlier in this chapter, older front-wheel-drive cars and some rear-wheel-drive cars can step out at the back if you lift off the throttle abruptly in mid-bend. This is more dramatic in wet conditions where the coefficient of friction between tyres and road is already reduced. In broad terms, what can happen is that, as you go round a bend and experience understeer, you may, quite correctly, attempt to remove it by gently lifting off your accelerator. Unfortunately, with these particular cars, if you are too quick to jump off the throttle in such a circumstance, you may instead precipitate an instantaneous, 'lift-off oversteer' skid. Although your front wheels may, at first, seem to tuck further into the bend, your back wheels may well be flung out sideways so abruptly that the initial understeer is more than cancelled out into oversteer. This oversteer will be much more difficult to control as explained earlier. So beware, be smooth and never panic.

With a few cars, especially some high performance ones, this transition from understeer to lift-off oversteer really does happen in a split second and is very treacherous. You then must stay off most of your throttle and apply counter-steering until grip is regained; directly you feel it returning you need gradually to reapply just the right combination of steering and throttle that should (hopefully) take you safely round the bend and out of trouble.

An expert would never risk the above possibility on a public road, even though knowing how to cope. It's too deadly dangerous. Regrettably, such is the speed of transition from understeer to oversteer, a novice can be caught off guard unwittingly, with a high chance of his car spinning on, out of control.

This surely is reason enough for all owners of high performance cars to undergo appropriate training on a race track or similar facility in order to familiarise themselves with the true handling characteristics of their cars.

If Your Car Spins

If your car spins, you must instantly accept that control has gone; then try to bring it back under control as soon as possible. You are usually best to brake as hard as possible and simultaneously de-clutch. Also, try to look around and see where your car may eventually end up. By de-clutching, you are able to keep the assistance of the brake servo and power steering – which would be lost if the engine stalled. By hitting your brakes, any friction between the sliding tyres and the road will have the effect of slowing the car, as will your interrupting of the drive to the wheels by de-clutching. At least these steps may give you some control of the outcome.

Unfortunately, recovering from a spin generally takes a lot of space and, on our narrow and crowded roads, it is unlikely that you will avoid a collision. However, by doing what you can to slow down, you do reduce the severity of any impact that occurs and if you regain some control you may be able to avoid other vehicles and anything too solid. It is far better to finish up on a grass verge than the wrong side of a brick wall!

Chapter 7:

Skills – No. 2 Braking

You would think that most drivers know how to brake properly, including in an emergency. Think again! Ninety per cent of road accidents involve a skid of some sort and poor braking skills are one of the major causes of skidding.

The importance of smooth, progressive, considered braking has been sadly neglected in recent years. Although almost a forgotten art, it is something we consider essential. In an emergency, the brakes have to be applied quickly and firmly, as well as smoothly and progressively; and using a consistently good technique *all the time* keeps you in tune for that critical moment.

Mostly, you should only need to brake much, in order to slow your car down, where engine braking and/or an uphill gradient will not do it for you. Whenever possible, brake on the straight, not when your vehicle is turning. This both maximises braking efficiency and retains vehicle stability and, therefore, safety.

For all these reasons (not to mention the comfort of passengers) smooth, progressive braking skill has always been one of the hallmarks of an expert driver. Sitting beside one, you can be astonished at how imperceptible his braking is in town or country. His car loses speed almost without you noticing it, so gentle is the transformation from power-on to brakes-on if needed. His return, via brakes off, to power resumed is equally jerk-free. Acceleration, feather-fed in, avoids the ragged transmission take-up characteristic of insensitive, amateur footwork.

Some drivers' progress seems constantly to be interrupted by heavy, jarring braking. This is a sign of poor forward observation or lack of concentration, leaving them too little time in which to react in a safe and considered way. For them, almost every other brake application becomes a partial emergency.

Driving Without Braking

If the above even remotely resembles your driving, consider this strange but true fact: avoiding *any* use of the brake pedal can improve not only your driving but also your braking skills! You should be able to drive many miles on B-roads without using your brakes at all. Perfecting this great skill makes you anticipate the actions of others and read the road at even higher levels of excellence, forcing you to get really involved in what you are doing. You save fuel and up-grade your attention to the road hugely. As a result, you will drive much more smoothly and build yourself an uncanny sense of timing. Of course, the need to use your brakes will happen but then you just start over again!

Braking Mechanics

Braking systems nowadays are very efficient and, under normal conditions, will pull you up in a straight line. How your car will behave under braking, especially heavier braking, depends on its design and the state of the road surface. You need to be very aware how it responds to specific braking pressures in different circumstances. A running brake test is essential with a car you have never driven before. It does not have to be dramatic – it is simply a matter of being aware of the feedback the car gives when you apply the brakes.

Learners are rarely given any chance to experience in their driving seats anything near emergency level braking from high speed. They cannot, therefore, begin to imagine, still less to visualise, the extraordinarily vast distances it can take to stop from top speeds as compared with stopping from some more modest pace. Yet, every driver needs a set of mind's eye pictures of the difficulties you can face. How else can you gauge safe following distances during fast driving until you know what can happen when the chips are down?

Whilst this chapter should expand your knowledge of braking at the theoretical level, we urge you, once you have absorbed it all, to test and build on your sub-emergency, braking ability; do so gradually up the scale of speed, choosing wide, safe, entirely traffic-free places (preferably dual carriageways if an off-road facility is not available to you) for this. You may need to get up in the early hours after dawn to find such places empty. Remember to use great care and your mirrors; you would only have yourself to blame should you cause an accident. (As the Highway Code formerly noted, you should never normally brake sharply except in emergency.)

This higher speed, hard braking practice may one day save your life. Work in stages in dry conditions first. Progress to semi-emergency brake testing on wet roads thereafter. Later, you will want to do the same on snow/ice when an opportunity arises. However, *high speed* on snow or ice, remember, has to be defined as any speed much over 15 mph.

Better by far, if you can find a suitable facility and have full permission and insurance cover, is to gain as much 'real' emergency braking experience as you can, off-road, including some genuine skids and some practical tests from high speeds. You need both dry and wet surface experience as well as on ice or equivalent conditions. Your aim is to know, ultimately, 'in your bones', what it really feels like to have to slam on your anchors from any speed and how to handle the consequences.

Always note:

- You exert maximum braking effect just prior to your road wheels locking up.
- When you double your speed you quadruple your braking distance;
- THAT DEMANDS *QUADRUPLING* YOUR SAFETY GAP AHEAD.

- Heavy loading (e.g. for holidays) makes for a vast reduction in your general control and ability to pull up swiftly.

Deceleration increases as you apply more pressure to your brake pedal until the point at which the wheels lock. As this happens and your tyres slide, retardation is at once reduced. Just before that point, your brakes are working at their maximum. Your best braking performance, therefore, is with your brake pedal pressure held on that level just before which your wheels lock, and where your tyres may be about to slip but are not yet actually skidding.

So, locking your wheels must be prevented wherever possible, because you have then passed the point of maximum retardation. At this same point, if it is your front wheels that have locked, you also lose your steering completely. Here is what happens on different road surfaces when you lock your front wheels:

- Dry road – locked front wheels give virtually maximum deceleration but you lose steering control. Also expensive as friction causes flat spots on your tyres.
- Wet road – locked front wheels greatly reduce maximum deceleration. Again, you lose steering control.
- Ice and snow – locked front wheels reduce deceleration even more. Again, your steering control disappears. (However, exceptionally, when ploughing into thick, unbeaten-down snow at *very* low speed, locked front brakes may finally stop you a little quicker, wedged as they can become against the built up snow.)

Your rear wheels can also lock. However, in a braking emergency, other than one first struck at comparatively high speed, this does not usually bode too much of a problem. Some four fifths of your braking effort mechanically depends and derives from front-wheel grip. As your vehicle weight impacts forward and downward under heavy braking, the load pushing down on your rear wheels is consequentially that much lighter. The tendency for those wheels to lock rather than grip is, therefore, increased. Whether or not this happens much during an emergency stop from moderate speed is normally relatively unimportant. Some skidding of your front wheels, rear ones or 'on all fours', may be unavoidable. Usually though, despite any minor skidding, you will stop in a pretty straight line.

However, maximum emergency braking from typical dual carriageway speeds of 50+ mph can prove savagely different if your rear wheels lock *first* and then slide sideways as well, as, sometimes, they will. (Thankfully, this generally will only occur if there is a vehicle defect.) This then becomes similar to oversteer, described in Chapter 6. Unless you are quick enough to reduce your braking so as to release those locked rear wheels, and to steer into the developing oversteer, this sideways skid can escalate rapidly into a spin, pivoting your car around your still partly gripping front wheels. The higher your speed at the outset, the greater the potential danger you can be in. (See page 103.)

During cornering, some of your vehicle's weight acts directly outward from the bend, counteracted by your tyre grip. This force, which your tyres must resist, is akin to that produced by a ball tied to a length of string and swung round in a circle, which effort will cause the ball to fly off if you let go or the string breaks.

Braking 'on-the-turn', to the point of skidding (i.e. tyre grip lost), lets that similar force take over; and, unless you know what to do next, you will 'fly' off the bend as a result. What to do was explained under understeer in Chapter 6.

Having to brake at all on a curved course stems from ineffective observation and a lack of advanced planning. If you absolutely must brake during cornering, then the brake pressure you dare apply must be curbed in relation to your steering angle at the time so as to prevent you simply careering onward, skidding simultaneously forwards and outwards. The higher the cornering force acting on your vehicle, the less braking potential you have. In other words, the more steering lock prevailing, the less the braking capacity remaining under your control.

The Right Way to Brake

For the best, smoothest results always apply your brake pedal gently. Tyres, suspension and passengers, too, are sensitive to drastic, violent braking forces. For example, a G-force of 0.3 applied suddenly is much more unsettling than a mighty 0.9 applied with smoothness and progression.

Expert braking has many advantages and no disadvantages. Try to practise the following techniques in your everyday driving:

- Always take up the free play in your foot pedal gently whilst you feel friction contact being established. You need to sense this initial 'bite' of your brakes and how your car's weight begins to be thrown forward, loading more force onto the front tyres and suspension. The less of a 'nose-dive' you create to start with, the smoother you will brake.

- Progressively increase your pedal pressure as required.

- Once down to the speed you want, reduce your pedal pressure, again progressively, not sharply. This way you will maximise vehicle stability and passenger comfort.

- Aim to create a flow throughout your whole braking process. If you are braking to a standstill, gently reduce your braking force just before your vehicle stops. This achieves a smooth, efficient and comfortable completion of the braking process and allows your suspension to recover in a controlled manner.

You can practise and refine the above braking skills nearly every time you touch the brake pedal. Become aware of how you brake in different situations. Give yourself a score out of ten each time, for smoothness and stability, and then think how you could improve your score. In a few weeks, this effort will bring impressive, everyday results. Your passengers will be astounded by the difference and you will have the satisfaction of achieving a tangible improvement in your driving skills.

Earlier Rather Than Later

If your observation and planning are up to scratch, emergency braking should be rare indeed. Undue frequency heralds tiredness. Should you stop and rest *now*? Otherwise it may be telling you (if only you will 'listen') that you need to drive slower, within rather than outside your current ability, and to learn to 'read the road' substantially further out ahead.

One Reason, One-Braking

For any specific need to slow down, the ideal is to make a single, smooth and sufficient brake application, releasing this with matching fluency as your speed drops to reach the level required. This will bring benefits you probably have never considered before. Vehicle stability, safety, control, passenger comfort and even your own satisfaction are all enhanced immeasurably by correct braking technique as it becomes a seamless part of your progress in the car.

Secondary Braking

However, here is a word of warning! Despite your best efforts, the amount of traffic on today's roads means you are bound to need occasionally to brake a second, or even a third, time.

If you need to brake then brake! We are all human and mistakes will occur.

Unfortunately, the result of several, significantly hard brake applications on the approach to, or whilst negotiating, a hazard is reduced vehicle stability. Therefore, such secondary braking should certainly be avoided whenever possible. Your car becomes a yo-yo with its mass moving backwards and forwards like a giant pendulum, and this is a sure sign of a non-expert driver who is not really in full control of his vehicle.

Do not fall into the same trap as one student on a police motorcycle course who, when he approached a bend, assessed the sharpness of the curve incorrectly. He braked to the speed he had judged to be correct but, as he got closer, realised this was still too fast. He knew that, if he applied his brakes a second time, the instructor following would see his brake light come on again. He decided to brave it out and tried to take the bend without secondary braking. He ended up in the hedge, fortunately with only the bike and his pride damaged!

If you do have to use your brakes more than once, well, learn from it. Ask yourself why? Did you assess the speed reduction required wrongly? Were you forced to brake a second time by the actions of another vehicle in front? Perhaps you were following too closely behind or your observation was not good enough? What could you have done to avoid the secondary braking and how can you avoid it in the future? Self-assessment of your everyday braking is, once more, the key to improvement.

Emergency Braking

Dealing with a braking crisis on a public road is one of the greatest challenges that any driver can face. Too often, the outcome depends on luck as to whether anyone chances to be in your way, unable to remove himself even if he sees you hurtling towards him out of control. The ability to do the right thing in a cool, calm and calculated manner in one of the most pressurised circumstances imaginable – when your life itself is suddenly and seriously threatened – lies mostly in the domain of those driving wizards whose control over mind and body is almost mystical. The fact that such drivers exist, however, shows what can be achieved, so let this be your motivation.

Your skill, knowledge and previous experience will inevitably be challenged by every new, braking emergency. As for any other living being, a sudden fright can strip you of your normal ability to co-ordinate thought and action in the first few seconds. Then 'panic-freeze' syndrome (see Chapter 6) can override all knowledge and leave you helpless and unable to cope. During a traffic accident, for instance, when things happen very quickly indeed, your inaction under stress can lead to a worsening of the outcome – as can any misguided action. In short, we all need to recognise that, when the crunch is nigh, we may not prove intellectually or emotionally up to dealing with an emergency. We may simply not know enough or not be able to put what we do know into practice sufficiently quickly and expertly.

Of these two emergency factors – knowing what to do and developing the ability to do it under extreme pressure – the first is the easier one with which to deal. This is mostly a question of training and experience where braking is concerned, and we shall start that process by explaining the right way to react, below. Your emotional control may be far harder to develop but this should not be impossible. The reality is that your emotions are much less likely to run amok once you have gained the right know-how. This is because fear of the unknown is thus largely removed.

Emotionally we are all different and our genes perhaps dictate the starting point in our ability to cope with stress. However, we can all improve and learn better to cope with an emergency. Clearly, you cannot on public roads safely or easily practise real braking emergencies which culminate with serious skidding and loss of control but, by learning and practising the correct ways to react, you can, at least, gain confidence and begin to take charge over your instinctive reactions, so lessening your chances of ending up in the clutches of a major, irrecoverable skid.

The only proper place to practise recovery from actual, severe, braking-induced skids is – as we have pointed out several times – on a skid-pan or a wet area specifically reserved for doing so in safety. There, you can learn to recognise and recover from most such skids so that, when you experience one in your daily driving, your 'instinctive' reaction will then be the correct one.

Self-assessment can also hone your ability to deal with crises. By becoming more aware of your underlying, temperamental reactions in an emergency, you should soon be able to modify your behaviour where necessary. Use any genuine, emergency braking incident as a learning opportunity. When your pulse rate has dropped and you have taken a few deep breaths, start to ask yourself about how you reacted. Did you see the cause of the emergency and react in time? Was your observation slow? Was your braking controlled? Did you manage to steer away from the problem? Whatever you do, avoid apportioning blame. Do not castigate yourself or others – we all make mistakes. The purpose of the questions that you ask yourself is to clarify what happened within yourself and thereby gain the chance to improve your future performance.

Having considered the right mental approach, you now need to return, if appropriate, to review the correct physical techniques and theory you require with standard brakes that are not computer-enhanced with an Anti-lock Braking System (ABS). These have all been set out earlier in this chapter.

The tricky skill, which needs a lot of self-control in a crisis, is to hold your brakes on the point of locking but without having them do so. In practice, the closest you will normally be able to get to this 'perfect' level of skill is known as cadence braking. The technique is well worth practising off-road so that, when a real emergency occurs, you will be better able to respond correctly.

Cadence Braking

On a slippery road, or one with a poor surface, cadence braking will normally make the most of what little tyre adhesion may be possible. It is not a perfect response but, with practised brain/foot co-ordination, it can enhance straight-line braking performance, and it can provide the best way to achieve at least some measure of control in a 'brake and turn' emergency manoeuvre. Should you ever lock your wheels on a dry road, the technique will come to your rescue there too.

Cadence braking is best described as a rapid, continuous and rhythmic pump-and-release action on the brake pedal – a sort of do-it-yourself anti-lock system (see next section on ABS). In the same way that an ABS automatically releases your brakes many times a second in order to let your wheels turn enough to preserve steering control, cadence braking allows you to steer to some degree (though not much) whilst simultaneously losing speed.

The technique is not as effective (or as easy to use) as an ABS, and the violent on-off braking can reduce stability. However, it is the next best thing and, if performed properly, cadence braking can work surprisingly well. Its skilful use may spell the difference between an accident and none.

The downsides of cadence braking are that it virtually requires you to lock your front wheels as part of the on-off-on-off cycle and that you can only steer whilst your brake pressure is released. In effect, you steer in between each downward pump of your brake pedal, i.e. when your road wheels are rotating.

This all reads in a more complex way than it soon becomes with a little, live practice. Why not give it a try the first time you can get an opportunity on a skid-pan? That is the place where you can most easily practise the skill in safety and without flat-spotting your tyres.

Overall, cadence braking maintains retardation and some steering control. The steering is applied and held steady but will only respond during brake release. What you are doing is braking, then letting the car steer. You may find it helps to shout 'pump – release; pump – release' to establish an effective rhythm. Ideally, you should pump your brake with this rhythmic action so as to keep in tune with the car's suspension movements: this way delivers the best control and curtails any undue loss of vehicle stability. The point to grasp as you learn this technique is that, although your downward strokes should be sufficiently hard to provoke momentary wheels' locking up, there is, when you are getting it right, no need to jump right off your brake pedal in between.

Braking/steering grip re-materialises at each wheel lock release and continues until it next locks and slides (i.e. skids). Therefore, all you want is to back off your brake pedal enough to regain rolling grip and make best use of this tenuous grip as your next down stroke immediately commences. If steering has to take priority at any stage, as it may in emergency, you might need to extend slightly a release phase whilst you grab some.

Emergency Braking with ABS

A survey among owners of vehicles fitted with Anti-lock Braking Systems (ABS) came up with a truly frightening statistic – more than 90 per cent of these drivers did not know how to operate their ABS properly in an emergency. Their working knowledge of it was hazy to say the least. They were variously confused about many questions such as these:

- What exactly is an ABS?
- What does it do and how does it work?
- Why have one?
- Does my driving need to change?
- How do I use it properly?
- Will it stop me skidding?
- Does it shorten or lengthen my stopping distances?
- Can I steer when using it?
- When might it make a situation worse?

Here follow the correct answers.

What is an ABS – How Does it Work?

An ABS prevents your road wheels locking-up under heavy braking and thereby retains steering control.

A wheel must revolve before it can steer a vehicle. Normally, a moving vehicle follows the path steered by its front wheels. If, in an emergency, you apply your brakes so hard that the brake pads grip the discs more strongly than your tyres can grip the road, then the wheels so affected will stop revolving and those tyres will simply skid across the road surface.

This is what happens without an ABS. Of course, it happens more readily when that surface is slippery. If it is your front wheels that lock, then, once they stop revolving, you simply skid onwards in whatever direction you were previously headed, rather than where you may have steered to go. Think of the familiar scene in many a Western movie when someone slides a glass along the bar in the saloon. The glass might spin as it slides but it always moves in a straight line. The same laws of physics apply to your car when its front wheels skid; you can turn the steering wheel as much as you like but it will have no effect on your direction. Under extreme braking, the same will happen if all your wheels skid at once. Should only or mainly your rear wheels skid, then you may suffer oversteer, an unpleasant affliction to which we referred earlier in this chapter and described fully in Chapter 6.

Remember that the friction between the tyre of a skidding wheel and the surface of a good, dry road is almost as great as it can be. Thus, in dry conditions, provided the road surface is not loose, you will normally stop in almost the same distance with any of your wheels locked as you would with them all held at the point just before locking.

The real advantages of an ABS, therefore, accrue in wet and treacherous conditions. Then the fractional friction you have left is much more difficult to harness.

Anti-lock brakes short-circuit the problems outlined above. They work their magic through having electronic sensors that constantly monitor the rotation speed of each wheel. During heavy or violent braking, these detect the point at which any particular wheel is about to stop rotating. The system then automatically and momentarily releases just enough pressure at the brake caliper concerned to prevent that wheel from locking. This takes a mere fraction of a second before the system reverts to full braking. If that wheel begins to lock again or any other wheel threatens to do so, it releases pressure once more in the right places to allow the wheel(s) in trouble to rotate – and so the process goes on: about to lock; release – about to lock; release ... The cycle happens over 15 times a second and you will sense it as a rapid clicking sound, usually also conveyed as a strong vibration through your brake pedal.

The system will carry on remorselessly until you have stopped or you release your brake pedal sufficiently for the ABS to cease working and for your brakes to revert to their normal, non-emergency mode (which is exactly the same as on non-ABS vehicles).

The system is hugely effective and the marvellous bonus it provides is that, for every alternate fraction of a second that your wheels are allowed to revolve, your car will also respond to your steering it. In practice that means you can still steer while braking as hard as possible at the same time. The sensors mostly remove the oversteer risk noted above, too.

However, it cannot be over-emphasised that, although an ABS should optimise your braking capacity on adverse surface conditions, it will not significantly reduce your shortest possible, dry-road stopping distances. If that comes as a surprise, please do not dream on. Neither should you rely on its superb benefits by closing up gaps or allowing your speeds to creep up despite tricky conditions. Just think of your ABS as adding a welcome, extra safety margin to the normal ones you must continue to maintain.

How You Use an ABS Properly in Emergency

Without question, Anti-lock Braking Systems have been one of the greatest lifesavers invented for motorists in years. In slippery conditions, no human can hope to match the high speed braking sensitivity and automatic compensating control these systems provide.

However, the lifesaving facility of an ABS can only pay dividends if you are able to steer clear of an accident in the heat of a dangerous moment. Just as the best way to overcome 'panic-freeze' syndrome (see Chapter 6) when you have standard brakes is to gain the right know-how to use them effectively when you're in danger, you should familiarise yourself to the same level with the extra know-how an ABS demands.

Again, the proper venue for this is an off-road facility on a wet day – preferably with use of a skid-pan thrown in. (See

Appendix.) Ideally, take a course there using an ABS to the full; you'll have a great time! If a course is out of the question due to cost, time or geography (although we would argue that achieving safety on the road is worth the trouble of overcoming such obstacles), you could try practising on your own. Find a stretch of tarmac off the public road where you can practise and will nonetheless be covered by your insurance. Failing that, find a deserted section of straight, dry road and, having ENSURED THAT IT IS TOTALLY SAFE TO DO SO, try a full emergency stop so that you see and feel what happens when the ABS cuts in. On safety grounds you probably won't be able also to practise steering under maximum braking – so save that for when you can find an off-road facility.

The major difference from non-ABS brakes that you simply must get your brain round is that, *in emergency*, you have to forget all you should have learnt about braking in terms of smoothness, progression, sensitivity, delicacy or the cadence technique. (Indeed, using the latter would cancel out what your ABS should do and make matters worse.)

With an ABS, you do not need them. Stop worrying about your wheels locking; your ABS deals with all that for you. This is what you do instead:

1. **Plant your brake pedal – VERY HARD**
2. **Keep it there**
3. **Look where you want to go**
4. **Steer there!**

Plant Your Brake Pedal – VERY HARD

Hit your brake pedal so hard you think your foot will smash through the footwell! 'Plant Your Brake Pedal – VERY HARD' is a key, colourful phrase by which to remember. Stamp really hard on it. The harder you push, the more ABS assistance you get.

Keep it There!

Do not lift off. Go on pushing as hard as you can until safety is obtained. As we warned above, any let-up can cancel your ABS assistance. The harder you can keep your foot down, the better.

Look Where You Want to Go

The major plus of an ABS is that you can still steer even though your foot is 'standing' hard on your brakes. So –

Steer There!

Look for a path to safety and steer for it.

An insight from motorcycle riding may instruct here: 'You go where you look.' Imagine, for a moment, riding along approaching a tight bend with limited vision. You lean your bike into the curve when, halfway round the corner, you see a house brick lying in the middle of your path. Clearly, you must avoid it. However, this won't happen if you continue to stare at the brick. That way, you will most likely hit it unless your master eye happens to be on the blink.

Instead you must look at the way round it that will keep you safe. Focus on your clear line, not on what you otherwise might hit.

'Panic-freeze' gauping at the brick is the classic, mesmerising error to turn on its head – now you know what to do.

Disadvantages of ABS

An ABS does have some disadvantages. For one it cannot make you a better driver than you were yesterday. Only you can do that. Nor is it foolproof – nothing ever is! Were it to fail (no backward thumping to be felt under your foot) you might need quickly to substitute cadence braking.

In heavy snow, an ABS may actually increase your stopping distance. The white stuff cannot build up into a wedge helping your final stop as it does with locked wheels – because your ABS prevents them from locking. This is why some ABSs can be disabled by means of a switch – ideal for Scandinavians frequently driving on fresh, unpacked snow.

ABS – Words of Warning

Take heed, in adverse weather, of your knowledge of ABS superiority. It may be fitted to the vehicle in front! Be realistic about its limitations. The final responsibility for safety lies with you, not your ABS if you have one. Various ABSs may display slightly different characteristics in operation, such as in the feedback feel of the brake pedal. However, these are insignificant in terms of their braking performances in action. What matters far and away more is that you develop the necessarily focused mental approach – underpinned by real know-how built up in your own driving seat – that will banish all trace of 'panic-freeze' when it really counts.

Chapter 8:

Skills – No. 3 Circuit and High Performance Driving

Learning from Racing Drivers

If you have ever driven on a circuit or watched racing drivers being ultra competitive, you will already realise that driving very quickly requires a great deal of extra talent, something akin to a sixth sense but very different. Have you ever wondered how racing drivers manage to gain an extra tenth of a second cut from a qualifying lap time, or to squeeze out every last ounce of cornering speed in a race?

Do you ever fantasise that road-driving skills alone might win you races? We can promise you they cannot. What, then, do motor racing drivers use and how do they produce those amazing feats of scintillating, quick driving and stay on the circuit, instead of sliding off into the gravel traps or the Armco barriers?

To become winners or, indeed, simply to compete at speed, they must learn a different set of rules and skills. Whilst this book does not attempt to cover the last words on how Formula One drivers go about their task, the elements contained in this chapter will give you a broad and expansive insight into the theory and practice behind driving very quickly. They should enable you to learn in new areas of skill and ability, and help you to understand how circuit-driving skills can make you a better and more knowledgeable road driver.

Fitness – Diet – Healthy Lifestyle

Do you ever see an overweight Formula One driver? Would a highly motivated, class-topping rally driver eat a huge meal or drink alcohol during the 48 hours before an event?

You certainly would not expect either to happen, would you? Neither would they ever be tolerated among so highly dedicated a bunch of drivers who know their lives depend on self-control.

Competitive driving at every level requires a different set of self-imposed rules and these boys stick to them without exception. Even at an amateur, hobby commitment stage, they must also live in a different world, and train along a hugely rigorous and demanding path, one that most of us cannot be expected to follow. That being said, many of their skills can be honed and made excellent use of in expert road driving.

Flexibility

Racing drivers have to be flexible to become top class. They add to techniques that we all use on the road – for example, changing gear, steering and braking – subtle differences in application which can be very useful in road driving. This flexibility in sharpening everyday expertise to new levels of precision, undreamt of by most ordinary motorists, is applied equally to the adoption (or rejection) of new and specialist racing techniques as they develop their experience. You need to develop such a flexible approach to your own driving skills and not merely mimic those set down in some driving manuals and advanced road-driving books. Engage your own brain, 'let in the clutch' and do the learning; there's no reason why you cannot become the inventor of some new and better concept or skill in road driving of which no one else has previously thought!

The 'traditionalist' advanced driver does not tolerate the use of such skills as 'heel-and-toe' braking with gear changing or 'fixed-input' steering, which we come to shortly in this chapter, even though they have been shown to be smooth and ultra-safe methods. Unfortunately, there lurk many 'traditionalists' in advanced driving organizations, members who have not moved forward from the set of skills they learnt many years ago. Why they are so inflexible and adopt such a 'dinosaur' attitude towards developing new driving skills – when traffic congestion, our roads and technology have changed so much – is something of a mystery. Many have never tried different skills and yet presume to sit in judgment on all of them.

So much of the new technology in road cars comes from racing car development, it seems madness not to analyse the skills being used and developed on the racetrack to see what can be learnt for road driving. The advantages in learning how to drive very quickly without crashing greatly outweigh any disadvantages, even though you would never use racing speeds on a public road. It is easy to get blasé about typical, 70 mph driving but the truth is you are then travelling very quickly indeed, and a lot of skill can be essential if things go wrong. Flexible learning and an openness towards the greater skills that may be used by other drivers should develop in you that level of expertise which can save you, and possibly many others, in dire emergency.

You will be able to adopt some of these skills into your everyday road driving and make the fullest use of their benefits. Usually, it will be by trying methods out quietly in safe conditions that you can judge with which skills to persevere and which do not work for you. In the end, it all improves your safety and enjoyment of driving – so do it!

Do not be put off by those traditionalist, so-called advanced drivers who, whilst they are very skilled and have much to offer, also have a 'head-in-the-sand' approach to anything new in the world of advanced driving. This mentality merely blocks out new skills that could improve their driving.

However, do not, either, dismiss all advanced driving courses just because of the views of some of the traditionalists. Much can still be learnt from them. Then, provided you discipline yourself against developing even a scintilla of a superior attitude, you will be more ready to move on and better your own expert driving, freed of any dogmatic or nonsensical, mental baggage.

Above all – keep safe! Each time you take the wheel remember it is you who must do this. Diplomas merely hang on walls; badges are prone to rust!

Fixed-Input Steering

This, like rotational steering discussed in Chapter 5, is very different from the standard, quite difficult, skill of 'pull-push' steering taught to learners and advanced drivers alike. Its purpose is to keep your brain more directly in touch with exactly how much steering lock you have applied during faster cornering in open-to-view conditions. Feedback 'feel' is enhanced and quicker reaction to the onset of any skid becomes possible.

You need to be holding your hands on your steering wheel for this as near to a (clock face) 'quarter to three' position as comfortably possible. You steer by turning the wheel with your hands in unison but *without shifting their wheel-hold position*. Keep a reasonably firm yet consciously relaxed grip. Tension creates a negative, non-sensitive feel which you need to avoid. Try to relax your shoulders (let them drop) and your arms at the same time, because this will help you achieve the relaxed mode most conducive to sensitive feedback signals being relayed properly.

Form a gently closed ring around your steering wheel rim with your thumb and forefinger. If your steering wheel has spokes at 9 and 3 o'clock, then you can also hook your thumbs around the cross spoke. However, be warned that, whilst doing the latter is fine for road and circuit driving, it must *never* be used when rally driving because the kick-back from the wheel on rough surfaces could easily break your thumb(s).

Thus, as you take a bend, the amount by which your hands have had to turn the wheel can never be in doubt; it's imprinted in your mind without any need for conscious thought because of where your hands have reached.

'What?', we hear you cry! 'Does this mean my hands,

respectively, can go past 12 o'clock and 6 o'clock without letting go?' Yes! You need to treat this as the 'exception that proves the rule' and free yourself of such archaic dogma. However, stay flexible! If your hands go much past 12 and 6 o'clock and the bend is still tightening up, you simply revert to 'pull-push' until the road straightens.

Straight ahead with thumbs and forefingers encircling the rim

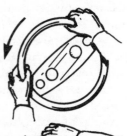

Turning left, your right hand moves up and your left down but neither hand moves its position on the rim

For more steering, your hands move further round.
If you need even more steering than shown, you have used the wrong steering technique for the manoeuvre

For turning right, you reverse the process

Fixed-input steering

Learn this fixed-input steering skill initially whilst driving straight. Progress to using it for cornering only when meeting wide and shallow bends, i.e. bends that you can see through well, and whilst traffic is light. The technique is _not_ intended for sharp, blind bends or slow speed manoeuvring. In those circumstances you could risk running out of available steering and that is not what being flexible or safe is all about. Your self-judgment counts for a great deal here. Choose fixed-input only for suitable opportunities. Switch back to 'pull-push' as the road configuration demands. Be careful to avoid confusion – which breeds dangerous indecision. If ever you consider that fixed-input might in any way be unsafe for a particular corner, stick to the basic 'pull-push' ingrained (we assume!) from the day you learned to drive.

So, with fixed-input, your hands move as one with the wheel. Let that gentle grip of the wheel between your thumb and forefinger perform most of the movement input; this helps maximize the amount of feedback you can accurately sense. Let your other fingers, held loosely around the steering wheel rim, act more as 'guides'. Only tighten them should this be necessitated – say by having to brake unexpectedly in the bend or when hitting ruts in the road surface.

Never allow fixed-input to impair your steering. Indeed, the opposite should be true; it should improve your technical performance because you are steering consistently with both hands and have the advantage of always knowing exactly where 12 o'clock is on the wheel, i.e. the dead ahead position. Some racing drivers and, particularly, rally drivers, have a piece of white tape on their steering wheel rims, placed – whilst the road wheels are precisely pointing dead ahead – directly at the 12 o'clock or top dead centre position. This, visually and subconsciously, reminds them where the straight-ahead steering position would be (_or is_), and where the front wheels are currently pointing. If you feel it helps, use one. Although we feel it is unnecessary for road driving, you may want to try it. (See what we meant about being flexible!)

Heel-and-Toe

Heel-and-toe is the old established, successful, motor-racing method of braking and changing down gear at the same time. Until someone thinks of a better way to achieve both simultaneously, it is likely to be around for a long time to come! Essentially, it allows you to lift your engine revs suitably up during continuous braking as you change down your gears on a manual gearbox. Done properly, it enables you correctly to realign your engine speed to that faster rate needed to match your road speed in the next gear down, at the precise point when your clutch release engages that gear. (It also prevents you ever re-engaging your clutch onto a 'dead engine' – i.e. an engine on tick-over speed. This can otherwise cause your drive wheels to lock-up if you do not use considerable care and delicacy.) Thus, heel-and-toe expertise promotes smooth, safe harmony in your vehicle's drive train whilst you simultaneously drop speed rapidly and re-gear for your next re-acceleration phase.

Although the word 'heel' is still used in naming the technique, your heel no longer plays any part in using it. It used to, years ago, but is not required at all in modern day racing cars or road driving, because the throttle and brake pedals are nowadays normally set quite close to each other. The relationship between their respective ranges of downward travel is also more appropriately aligned. The word 'toe' is almost equally redundant because it is the two sides of your right foot that you now mostly use. To explain further, in the early days of motoring, foot controls were set some distance apart. This meant that your heel could be placed on the throttle and your toe on the brake – though not without some difficulty! The method, if done incorrectly, lacked sensitivity because your foot had to be placed at such an unnatural angle. By contrast, in most modern vehicles, very sensitive control – vital for driving at or near the limit – can be achieved relatively easily. It is one reason why racing drivers generally have very thin soles on the undersides of their shoes or racing boots. Touch and feel become important, if not vital.

To perform heel-and-toe you must teach your right foot to work your throttle and brake simultaneously. Furthermore, your right foot must be attuned to maintaining its even (or, more usually, progressive) pressure on your brake pedal, through its middle and left side, at the same time as it manipulates your throttle, up or down, as required, through its remaining, righthand part. This is quite a tall order for which you will need extensive practice well away from other traffic to begin with.

You need to position your right foot so that its main body is on the brake pedal and only the lesser, righthand part is ready to manipulate the throttle pedal. You must never risk slipping

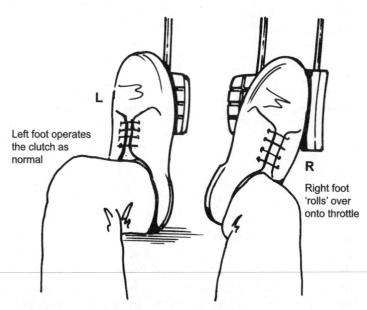

L

R

Left foot operates the clutch as normal

Right foot 'rolls' over onto throttle

Depending on the pedal layout, your right foot 'rolls' over when applying the throttle whilst still applying the brake. Different pedal layouts will require slight adjustment of your right foot position

Heel-and-toe techniques

off your brake because your foot is too far over towards your throttle. Bear in mind also that braking almost invariably requires more effort than using your throttle.

The correct placement of your foot is perhaps the paramount skill with heel-and-toe. Whilst your ability to brake at the utmost pressure dare not be jeopardised, neither can you afford any possibility that the righthand edge of your shoe might slip below, or even lodge under, your accelerator pedal. Because of this, you may need to make a careful choice of footwear. Some readers may have to accept that, for example, they should not attempt the technique when wearing thick-soled trainers or shoes.

Others may even need to forgo heel-and-toe altogether, if the set-up of the pedals in their cars proves inappropriate or their feet are simply too small.

Smoothness when re-engaging your clutch is the other piece of nifty footwork skill that can make or mar successful use of heel-and-toe. When also timed to perfection, this produces flowing, seamless gear changes, sublimely accomplished, and which harness the added safety of engine-braking control directly into your speed reduction – with your engine and gearbox always mating in exquisite symmetry.

There are two alternative methods of throttle adjustment when using heel-and-toe during continuous braking. In the first, as you begin braking, you also position the righthand part of your right foot above (but off) your throttle. Your engine revs can therefore continue to fall until you have de-clutched for dropping down to your next gear. After selecting that gear, you 'blip' your throttle in time and in measure sufficient, so that – during the period in which the extra revs die away – you will be able to 'catch' just the right amount of their increased rate that will match your falling road speed in your new, lower, gear as you let your clutch smoothly back in. The trick here, which takes the most practice, is combining your throttle 'blip' with unbroken, even (or progressively harder) braking – unaffected by the dual role of your right foot.

In the second ('sustain') method, having already begun

braking and positioned your right foot as for the longer-established method detailed above, you now use that right-hand part of your right foot on your throttle at the point of your de-clutching for gearing down. Your objective is to 'sustain' your engine revs from this point so that they fall no further. Indeed, you may need to make them rise slightly, to the required level for the lower gear, by careful adjustment with that righthand part of your foot − so that they can be 'sustained' at that level whilst you select your lower gear and let your clutch in to engage it.

We prefer the 'sustain' way as it usually proves the easier one to apply consistently. It is also smoother when perfected − although you must be careful not to depress your throttle until your drive is fully disengaged, otherwise you would be trying to brake and accelerate at the same time! Again, it takes a lot of practice to be able to get the revs up to, and not over, the required level, at the same time as selecting the lower gear. All this must be achieved before your clutch release. You must then gently lift off your throttle in order that engine braking can be resumed.

In racing or rallying, you grasp maximum retardation when braking, by going down through each gear in turn, say, for example, from 5th to 4th to 3rd, on your way into a moderate chicane. In the same way, a heel-and-toe technique, down through each of the gears concerned, can be really advantageous during a brisk drive through quiet country lanes − where you may wish sometimes to leave braking for a bend a little later than usual but, nevertheless, still arrive in the correct gear and at the perfect speed for going round and exiting the bend. This apart, the general rule for road driving is to use only one brake application and one gear change on approach to any specific hazard. However, the heel-and-toe technique suits both occasions equally well and so forms an important link in the chain of skills an expert driver wants to maintain.

You can also 'blip', or 'sustain' your way down your gears, without combining that with any braking at all. This 'half-way house', gaining mostly the bonus of engine braking control, really comes into its own on snow or, particularly so, on ice. There, your only hope of slowing or stopping – even from suitably low speed for these conditions – may depend on a seamless, entirely jerk free, going down of your gears because even a light touch on your footbrake provokes a skid.

We recommend that you experiment with all gear changing skills, including the old fashioned 'double de-clutch' method, so that you are fully conversant with every technique. Indeed, if you get the opportunity to drive a veteran or historic car you will find that double de-clutching is a must on all gear changes, because there is usually no synchromesh in the gear-box and your revs have to be matched pretty exactly to your next gear. Just to remind you – in order to double de-clutch *going down the gearbox* you firstly depress your clutch whilst throttling back and exiting gear into neutral. Then raise your clutch fully, before 'blipping' your throttle as you put your clutch down again. The trick now is to select your next gear down quickly enough before those revs die away (or your gear cog wheels will 'graunch' out loud!) and for those revs still to be on board as you engage the gear by smoothly letting your clutch back out again – with engine, new gear and road-wheel speeds all harmoniously matched. Alternatively, as with heel-and-toe, you can 'sustain' the revs whilst activating the clutch and selecting your new gear.

Drivers who have developed heel-and-toe skill can combine its added sophistication with these downward, double de-clutching gear changes.

Double de-clutching *up your gears* is easier. Heel-and-toe would not be relevant, and you do everything the same except without the throttle blip during that intermediate, clutch fully up phase; a momentary pause is all you need there – engine idling as it will anyway without throttle.

Balanced Throttle

This is another technique you can learn from racers. 'Balanced throttle' is a descriptive term for correctly setting up the various forces acting on your car whilst cornering. The first rule is 'the smoother you are, the quicker and safer you are'. This applies absolutely to dealing with your car's inertia, moving mass and weight distribution, all of which inter-react and demand your close attention from the time you enter a bend through until after leaving it. In racing, where the car is being driven on the limit of adhesion, any lack of cornering smoothness quickly leads to a spin, a crash, or a trip into the 'kitty litter'. Knowing best how to set up just the right balance on entry, and then provide exactly the correct inputs to maintain and exploit that equilibrium throughout the remaining course of, and exit from, the bend, is what marks the difference between a good racing driver and a great one.

What you do with the 'balanced throttle' technique is the same for both racing and road driving. Any differences are simply of degree and reflect mostly how close to physical limits may be appropriate in each instance. On approach to any bend you must pre-judge a safe, final entry speed, brake if needs be, and drop down to the gear you assess will best suit taking the bend itself. All this must be completed prior to steering into the bend. Ideally, that completion – by now on trailing (zero) throttle – will shortly coincide with reaching your 'turn-in' point. Immediately prior to 'turn-in', you restore just enough power (throttle) to even out those forces which will then act on the car from the moment you steer in.

When you are braking, the weight of your car is being thrown largely over your front wheels; under hard acceleration, it shifts and is forced more towards the rear. You feel this happening and, by applying just sufficient power, aim to even out that weight redistribution so as to progress through the apex of the bend on an even keel – with neither nose, nor tail, down. Once you begin to straighten up at the end of the bend, you move on from 'balanced throttle' and apply more power. How much must now depend on how quickly you are able to reduce your steering angle. You are at a delicate stage of balance and don't want to shift your vehicle's weight too sharply from its front or mid point of exertion further towards the rear. Once straight, just moments later, you can put your foot down for full speed if you wish. Your car's weight will then act mainly pressing down on your rear wheels – which is fine for straight-ahead driving. However, you must still take care, in wet or slippery conditions, not to apply too much power at once as you re-enter the straight.

Once you perfect 'balanced throttle', bends become almost imperceptible, even though you may be travelling quite quickly; whereas you will notice poor balance instantly, because your car at once seems to be lurching all over the place.

Smoothness and balance are the hallmarks of an expert driver. Practise them all the time. Awareness of the exact inputs your car needs to corner efficiently grows with practice but diminishes all too rapidly once neglected.

On-the-Limit Braking

Racing cars do not have ABS as the governing bodies who rule the sport currently outlaw them. So the drivers have to compensate for this by learning to use various 'on-the-limit braking' skills. All of these require you to sense the feedback from your brake pedal and develop a 'feel' for what your car is doing. They include threshold braking, cadence braking, interference braking and, sometimes, even locking your wheels when braking.

Threshold Braking

Threshold braking, if you can manage to apply it in emergency, is a most useful and potentially lifesaving skill. As you already know, on any vehicle without an ABS, the ideal way of braking in an emergency is to be able to hold your pressure on your brake pedal at the point just before the wheels begin to lock. This yields maximum braking and without loss of steering control.

Threshold braking is exactly that – you hold your brake pressure at the point just prior to wheel lock, and we mean *just* prior. Some racing drivers achieve this by first locking the brakes (even if imperceptibly) and then releasing a fraction of the pressure to get the road wheels rotating again. This is the easy way and, some would say, 'cheating'. However, it is so difficult to apply the correct pressure to reach threshold that most drivers have to resort to the easier way. Only the most skilled can hit the threshold spot with precision – without first locking and then releasing, ever-so-slightly, their road wheels.

We suggest that you only attempt to gain this skill at a race or rally driving and skid training facility in a car provided for the purpose, because you will undoubtedly flat-spot your tyres if you use your own car. Besides, this impressive technique is most certainly more safely learned away from the public road.

Cadence Braking

Described by Chapter 7, this is the most certain method of emergency braking (particularly in slippery conditions) for most drivers who do not have an ABS. If that is you, think of it as your 'default' mode unless you have become a total master of one of the other methods presented by this chapter – *and* that method is also the most appropriate to the emergency in hand.

Interference Braking

This last-resort skill is almost completely unknown, even amongst expert drivers. The only time you would use this very specialist technique is when facing an emergency evasion manoeuvre, say, around a stationary obstacle ahead. It's not feasible with an ABS-equipped car because it depends on locking your wheels.

With interference braking you hit your brakes hard enough to produce total wheel lock. As you slide on, wheels locked, ever closer towards whatever you are desperate to avoid, you must put on, approximately, a quarter turn of steering, left or right, whichever way safety lies. Now steel yourself to hang in there until the last moment you dare – when sudden release of your brakes should make your car swerve clear round the obstacle.

Of course, you will have read the above paragraph in slow motion in comparison with how quickly it all has to happen in a real event. Top racing drivers would reserve this skill, for example, to avoid another competitor stopped, blocking the racetrack. Its use in emergency on a public road would undoubtedly demand supreme presence of mind and, probably, a great deal of previous mock experience of it in the safety of a suitable proving ground.

Locking the Wheels Whilst Braking

Most experts agree that, technically, the quickest way to stop a car without an ABS *in dry conditions* is to hit your brakes as hard as you can. This obviously causes total wheel lock yet, in a straight line, you will stop quicker than with cadence braking. Steering loss won't matter where you have a straight line available, though you will flat-spot your tyres. However, that will be a small 'price' if it saves an accident. Whether you would have the mental agility to choose this alternative over cadence braking, in the heat of trouble, is another matter. Unless you have such confidence, stick, as we have suggested, with cadence braking as your first emergency plan, so that you can also concentrate on where to steer to avoid a collision.

Trail Braking

Up to now we have always advocated that you do not brake in a bend if it can be avoided. However, it is possible to balance your car on your brakes in the early part of a bend (albeit a touch nose down) and then switch, skilfully, to pick up that balance again on your throttle exactly at the right moment. The advantage is that you can brake further into the bend, and set yourself up with your throttle for going round at a slightly later stage – as the bend unwinds in front of you. In this way you will be able correctly to assess your speeds for individual bends on a more consistent basis. Traditional cornering requires that speed for a bend be judged at an earlier stage, when less of the bend can be seen.

Your switch from brakes to throttle must be done at, or just before, the apex of the bend. After the apex you will need to be holding the car on the throttle ready to accelerate away as the bend opens up. This changeover takes a lot of skill and must be learnt away from public roads, preferably with an instructor in the initial stages.

Racing drivers use trail braking extensively, as it gains the advantage of carrying more speed into a bend – as it indeed means that they can leave their braking to the very last split second. However, even they have to practise and practise before the technique becomes second nature, with no risk of losing balance in mid-corner.

The skill is rarely taught other than to highly skilled, advanced road drivers because it needs a great deal of 'feel' and the ability correctly to assess the feedback felt through your car's controls and the 'seat of your pants'. Blindly to hammer on your brakes heading into a corner is asking for trouble. You need to exercise a high degree of judgment, advance observation and skill.

As with normal cornering, the majority of your braking must still be done on the approach but, instead of initially picking up the balance of your car with your throttle, you will appreciate that it will be your brake release that first causes weight to be lifted from your front wheels. You continue your braking (relatively gently by the time of arrival), right through your steering 'turn-in' and towards the apex. As you reach the apex you ease the last of your brake pressure and only subsequently restore some throttle to pick up the remaining balance you will need. That places you in readiness for further acceleration as you regain the straight.

Trail braking is ideally suited to be used in conjunction with heel-and-toe downward gear changes because your braking can continue smoothly throughout. Again this combination of skills can only be safely learnt away from the public road. (See Appendix.)

Pause for breath if the last few pages have raised in you a tingle of excitement that says 'I can't wait to give some of these techniques a go!', and reconsider our words of warning.

In the main these are NOT methods to acquire by trial and error on public roads. You need coaching in the safe hands of an experienced instructor on a dedicated track or proving ground.

More important still, if you do master some or all of them, is the self-discipline that must restrain your road driving from the sort of excessive speeds that might cause you to have to extricate yourself from an emergency you would not otherwise have got yourself into.

You become a dangerous maniacal driver, no matter how much you may try to rationalize and excuse your behaviour, the moment you step over the above line and risk – on a public road – any speed from which you cannot still stop fully under control and within the safe distance you can see to be clear. Furthermore, acquisition of these skills does not remove your obligation always to consider the safety of other road users.

The Real Experts

When it comes to 'feel' and balance, racing and rally drivers are generally in a different league from most road drivers. The best have a supreme knack for understanding what is happening with a car stretched close to its limits under maximum acceleration, braking or cornering forces, or almost any combination thereof. They can sense whether or not their cars can be coaxed to go two or three miles per hour faster round a specific bend on a circuit without too much sliding. Faced with understeer or oversteer they feel it instantly, and react faster; this to make minor adjustments on the controls so that they can hold their cars at the point of maximum speed without 'getting out of shape' from the line being driven. They are every bit as slick to recognise even the remotest of slides at the front or rear and counteract with instantaneous, minute adjustments to their speed as necessary.

They are also able to articulate to the engineers where mechanical improvements/adjustments can be made to achieve an optimum set-up with the car. Their reward comes with the incredible speeds at which they become capable as well as safe, often tuned specifically to the track and conditions prevailing; speeds that the normal driver cannot really comprehend.

This level of skill does not come with one or two races. Remarkably few ever get to such a stage in their personal development but, those that do, will always have the edge over the others and thereby win races.

Whilst racing drivers need rare talent in this regard, the ultimate champions of chassis 'feel' and balance are, without question, test drivers. Their job is to assess and evaluate a car's chassis characteristics and behaviour. They then tune its steering, suspension and braking to achieve the best overall performance. They are highly skilled individuals who seem to 'just know' what a car will do when they make even a minor input into the steering, throttle, or brakes. They have developed an apparently in-built, 'sixth sense' about it all and, if you ever get the opportunity to sit alongside one when he is working, you will find it an experience to savour once your nerve resurfaces!

Once again such skills are not learnt in a year or two. Years are needed to reach the top of this class. These are also the drivers who can hold a car hurtling along on a test track in total control when, by all appearances to the layman, they have lost it. At the same level, normal drivers simply take fright and brake but not test drivers. They have the ability to take total charge over their emotions and never panic – a mental state called 'emotional stability'. They are not fearless but do possess this extraordinary degree of mental control. This combines with a superlatively educated 'instinct' for when delicate and minute adjustments must intervene to maintain equilibrium and prevent the car from leaving the track in a fair hurry. Many have been trained to be test drivers but only the most dedicated and talented make the top grade.

We cannot all reach such supreme heights of expertise but you do need to develop a good 'feel' for the balance of your car to become an expert driver. Much is to be gained by close attention to the feedback your car is giving you. Keep asking yourself what the effect was of the input you gave to the car in particular circumstances. Did your throttle input help balance, or make it worse? Did your insensitive braking unduly disturb stability? Could you have timed your steering better? You must dedicate yourself to this continual-reappraisal style of thinking if you are to improve and maintain that improvement. The average driver, regrettably, ignores much of what the car is saying in terms of feedback and learns little. Expert drivers use all their senses, stay totally aware, and continue to learn. There is nothing wrong, either, with giving yourself a little praise when it's due for good performance; so long as you remember that this won't last unless you go on making this effort to keep it so.

Using Track Skills in Road Driving

Many of the racing and rally skills in this chapter can be used in road driving. Whilst we have seriously warned against any abuse of them on public roads, it is important to appreciate how the knowledge of them can often form the basis of that greater level of understanding usually only seen among genuinely advanced road drivers.

If a certain skill improves your driving, or indeed helps you to avoid an accident, then it will have been worthwhile learning and honing. You never know when that expert skill might be called upon in an emergency but, when it is, it may save your life or the lives of others. So never presume that areas outside your present knowledge of driving cannot make you a better driver or that you have nothing to learn from them. They all have some part to play in developing in you the expert driver, provided you stay sufficiently self-aware, flexible and open-minded – more especially, sometimes, because of negative feedback – in other words, what you can learn *not* to do again.

Chapter 9:

Adverse Conditions

Road conditions vary enormously and change fast. An expert driver rapidly identifies deteriorating conditions and makes skilled adjustments to his driving for dealing with them.

Wet Roads

Correctly inflated tyres give excellent adhesion in the wet most of the time. However wet-road grip will never be as good as in dry conditions, and the presence, on top of any wet surface, of mud, wet leaves, oil, or diesel slicks, may dramatically exacerbate the risks presented by wetness alone. Worn road surfaces, when wet, can also precipitate very slippery conditions that can catch you out. Overall speed reduction, increased vehicle spacing and more gentle use of your throttle and brakes are essential but ignored by too many.

A slightly damp road results roughly in a 15 to 30 per cent loss of adhesion for which you must allow. It will take proportionately longer to stop and you will have a similar loss of steadfast cornering ability. The effects sometimes appear to be worse until a road has been 'washed' by heavier rain. However, generally, as a road gets wetter so the levels of adhesion continue to decrease a little more. Look out for any extra greasiness, for example, from engine oil droppings where traffic frequently has to stop.

Rain mixed with a diesel spill can reduce tyre grip to almost nothing and is not always easy to detect by eye. Leaked diesel is usually caused by overfilling of tanks by unthinking drivers. So

Wet conditions demand advanced observation and early planning

beware close to filling stations and at nearby traffic lights or roundabouts – favourite spots for the excess to slop over.

Chapter 6 goes into, in some depth, what to do should you skid. The corrective actions are essentially the same, wet or dry. It's the threshold at which skidding forces get the upper hand that drops so very considerably when roads get wet.

Advanced observation and earlier Driving Plans (see page 49) will help you distinguish any areas of the road surface that require special attention and thereby to arrive well-prepared to reduce any danger. Look for wet patches under trees and by tall hedges, where the sun may have been prevented from drying the road surface. Take note how some trees exude residues onto the road which become exceptionally slippery when damp. After heavy rain take extra care on roads where water may be streaming across from one side to the other or where flooding may have yet to subside. This occurs quite frequently on country roads and can be very dangerous when come across quickly on a bend or a dip and, in darkness, the possible consequences hardly bear thinking about. (See Chapter 6.) Aquaplaning is an ever-present risk in such conditions.

Bright Sunlight

In a low winter sun you can find yourself fighting to find a place to look forward where your eyes are not blinded instead of observing the road hazards all around. Always have sunglasses available and, as with all difficult conditions, slow down as necessary to preserve safety levels. Be warned that very strong sunlight can play tricks with drivers' vision, too, making flashing indicators and brake lights much harder to notice, especially when, up ahead of you, they first come on.

Use your sun visor but still be ready to move your head should the sun start to streak through the gaps around it, as indeed it will, for example, on a curving motorway stretch. Be ready, in that circumstance, for rapid slowing down as others in front of you are sure to suffer temporarily blinding rays too. On winding, narrow roads you may have the sun directly behind you from time to time. Keep a closer watch on oncoming drivers when this happens; they may stray into your path unintentionally – half a second's distraction for them can be enough to cause you both an accident.

Ice and Snow

Your best safety device on these is the judicious use of your right foot!

A highly developed sensitivity and smoothness on your controls is the principal secret of maintaining tyre grip in such conditions. You will be wise to keep below 20-25 mph and much slower in trickier places. Change your speed, up or down, ever-so-gently, and only a little at a time insofar as you are able; steer gently.

Our Chapters 6 and 8, between them, said much about skidding on wet roads. All of that applies very specifically in icy and snowy conditions, except that, on ice and snow, the skid threshold is substantially lower because grip is so much reduced. This threshold is also usually much more variable – being quite capable of dropping to almost zero speed here and there or, indeed, sometimes, everywhere. Keeping your speed right down may make you feel you will have more time to respond but stopping distances, particularly on ice, are far longer than most drivers expect. You can take ten times further, or more, to stop on ice than in dry conditions.

Advanced observation, planning and the preservation of adequate stopping room are absolutely critical in these conditions. The latter factor must govern your choice of speed at all times. Each stage of your Driving Plan(s) (see Chapter 4) must come that much earlier to allow for it.

You should aim to stay in the *highest gear* that will take you forward without wheelspin on the one hand, or with your engine always being about to stall on the other. Generally, use your throttle and gears to slow down, not your brakes – which can trigger a locked wheels' slide all too easily. (Hold on your brakes when stopped.)

When you see ahead that you will probably have to stop, make a light brake test well ahead of where that stop needs to be, so as to assess how much stopping ability you are likely to find you have when you get there. This should tell you where to begin your actual slowing process, if it is to be made safely in good time.

Sometimes packed down, iced-over snow becomes so slippery that merely turning your steering wheel is enough to induce a skid. Take this as a signal that even walking pace may now be too fast.

When conditions are this bad a steeply cambered road may carry you on an ignominious slide into the gutter, a slide that once begun is hard to stop. Before a stretch of this sort of road, slow down or stop; wait until a cessation of oncoming traffic will allow you a clear run well out from the edge. Do the same before any steep hills. You neither want to have to stop and start again halfway up a hill – nor to find you cannot physically stop at all, going down, perhaps placing both yourself and others in great danger. Going up a steep hill, incidentally, select and engage a gear that should take you all the way up without having to change gear again. Making such a gear change half-way up can dissolve all traction, leaving you with your driving wheels spinning away but making no progress.

Start from rest on snow in 2nd gear, or possibly 3rd, slipping your clutch as necessary so as to avoid spinning your wheels. Listen and feel for that because, once begun, you usually only dig in more. Stop. Try reverse for a moment – then forward on the rebound; and repeat as necessary to get you out with a 'rocking' motion. Failing that, helpers, pushing your vehicle *without the engine*, may well prove more effective for getting you out than having you spinning your wheels whilst they try. Furthermore, if you remembered to put that shovel in the boot, digging away the worst of the snow should get you going.

Virgin snow can easily catch you out if you are not careful. You will have control all the time your tyres can bite through the fresh snow and maintain some contact with the road surface. The same happens in slush. However, should you

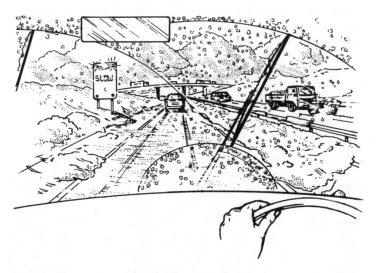

It will take far longer to stop in snow conditions

increase your speed too much, the amount of snow/slush to be dispersed by the tyre quickly becomes too great and your tyres part company with any grip. Your resulting skid will be serious because you will have already overstepped any safety margin of speed you might have had.

Snow can soon be rutted and the ruts have the effect both of holding your car on line and then throwing it off line unexpectedly; so be careful.

Some types of ice are very hard to detect. They don't glisten and some masquerade as wet surfaces, especially at night; so, always be cautious and hold your speed right down when freezing point approaches. Carry out occasional light brake tests in suspicious conditions (but only at slow speeds); then you should be among the first to know trouble is at hand. If it has been raining just before the freeze sets in or there is what weathermen describe as 'freezing rain', then this is the recipe for black (unseen) ice. This is probably the most difficult adverse condition with which to deal. Walking pace may prove too fast. A skid once started may not end except with a bump!

Slippery conditions, however they are caused, are likely to provoke anxiety and, as a result, tension in the hands and arms. This is exactly what you do not want because a light grip, and the sensitivity to 'feel' the constantly changing slipperiness, are what are required. To stay safe it is hugely advantageous to keep relaxed. Confidence that enables this comes through quickly gained awareness and experience. Open a window on both sides of your car and use your ears. They can tell you when wet switches to ice because, suddenly, your car runs more quietly.

The best way to gain the essential experience, however, is on a skid-pan. Most types of skid can be simulated, so that you can learn how to recognise them and correct them yourself. Treat yourself to a session on one if you haven't already done so. They are enormous fun as well as being a great learning experience. The Appendix should help you locate a venue. Should you find yourself in Scandinavia during the winter then consider joining an ice-driving course at one of the local driving schools. This is a truly exceptional way to learn to drive on ice and snow, albeit on studded tyres.

Fog and Bad Visibility

In fog and other poor visibility, most people still drive too fast for their own ability. How many horrendous motorway accidents do we need to have before drivers wake up and accept this, and drive accordingly? Awareness is, once again, the secret of preserving safety. The density of fog varies deeply; equally, it follows that you must continually be revising your speed in order to match that fast-changing depth to the amount you can still see, ever relating it moment-to-moment, to how far you need to stop dead if you have to.

By day as well as by night, use dipped headlights and/or fog lights, plus rear fog lights. Half the battle is to make sure you are *seen*. However, you don't want to use main beam on your own headlights. This will often make visibility worse in foggy conditions – more especially in the dark – because the light is reflected back from the water droplets of the fog into your eyes.

Take great care where the fog is patchy. This is a particular problem on motorways, where it can be clear one moment, and then the next you are immersed in a thick blanket of the stuff. If you are alert and looking ahead, you should be able to spot the worst bits before you reach them, and slow down in advance accordingly. Be prepared for those following behind not to be so aware. Check your mirrors and be ready, with a light touch on your brake pedal, to flash your brake lights if traffic closes on you as you slow down. However, try not to overuse your brakes – and thus your brake lights – or you run the risk of having them ignored.

In very thick fog it is easy to become disoriented. Look for recognisable signs, such as road markings, traffic signs and street-light patterns. Open your window and listen. Valuable clues can sometimes be heard when not seen! If conditions get really bad then you have no choice but to find somewhere safe, well away from any main carriageway, to park and stop for a break until the conditions ease.

If fog is likely, try to complete your journey before dark because visibility in fog is dramatically reduced by darkness. Your main visual focus should be as far as you can see up the edge of the road on your side but do not dwell on this aspect alone. Most importantly, look at what you *can* see rather than strain your eyes into the murk where you cannot see anything. A feeling of unease about how much you really are seeing ahead warns you to *slow down more*.

Eyestrain in fog or driving snow can quickly cause fatigue and make you a less efficient driver, just when you need to be on top form. Do not allow your eyes to become transfixed on the blankness of the fog ahead. Keep them moving and scanning for such items as stationary vehicles parked at the side of the road, cyclists and pedestrians. Remain fully aware of vehicles behind. Some drivers close up in fog so as to keep visual contact with the vehicle in front of them. This is both alarming and dangerous. An expert driver will be very circumspect about following suit, other than from an exceptionally respectful distance. Do frequent mirror checks and allow for this situation in your planning.

PLEASE stick to the law and switch off rear fog lights as soon as visibility improves. They irritate drivers behind you and may mask the effectiveness of your brake lights. Also, PLEASE do not become an illegal nuisance by using front fog lights in clear conditions. They only distract and annoy oncoming traffic.

Night Driving

Even the best headlights cannot compare with daylight. Less vision, to an expert driver, equals less speed, so you can never travel as fast at night as during the day. You must, just as by day, relate your speed to the vision available. Although you will see further with the main beam of your headlights, it is not usually long, on our crowded roads, before you have to dip them and so reduce your length of vision considerably. Your driving speeds must never rise too high to cater for this abrupt change. Think of your throttle as if it were connected to your dip switch, and drive accordingly.

Use main beam when the road ahead is clear: firstly, you can then plan further out ahead – you will see the whites of pedestrians' eyes, for example, not yet visible on dipped beam; secondly, oncoming and/or potential crossing traffic gets earlier warning of your approach; and thirdly, you will assist drivers wishing to overtake you by lighting their way for them.

When you drive, you depend very heavily on sight but, at night, much of the information you use by day is no longer available. Human beings are very sight-dependant, especially when they drive, and so night driving can cause anxiety for many people. The secret is to remain alert and gather all the available information even though it is more limited at night. Cultivate a high level of awareness, for example, of the anxiety just mentioned occurring amongst fellow road users, and take account of all the little tell-tale signs of life that you can see. One such sign might be the sudden appearance of twinned (close together) headlights in your mirrors, rather than pairs set apart normally. This is probably a motorcycle that may pass you any second.

Make sure your eyesight is good and have it checked if you feel it is adversely affected by night driving. Be most particular about keeping all your car windows and mirrors clean and demisted.

In twilight you want to be seen, so be among the first to put on your headlights. This will also encourage others. If driving into dawn, be among the last to switch them off. Use headlights not sidelights – as all road users, including pedestrians and cyclists, can see them more readily.

Safety Systems and Features

Devices that help keep you safe in adverse conditions are becoming ever more sophisticated but responsibility for primary safety (i.e. avoiding accidents) remains with you, the driver. These systems increasingly make cars far safer, feel safer and generally easier to drive. It is worthwhile knowing about some of them even before they reach standard equipment status on popular, less expensive cars. We highlight some of the more interesting of these developments in the next few pages.

Brake Assist

This is a relatively new safety-oriented braking device that is controlled through ABS sensors. When the device detects that the driver is applying more pressure than usual on the brake pedal, it takes over and applies full braking effect until he relieves sufficient pressure on the pedal. Vehicle manufacturers have found in the past that many or even most drivers, in emergency braking situations, either do not brake hard enough or they release their brakes too early. It is safe to say that many drivers are likely to lack confidence in such wizardry; yet, this device can be very effective in braking correctly in a real-life, emergency situation encountered on the road. Perhaps we all need to have more faith in the manufacturers who, with products such as these, generally do not get it wrong. Brake Assist is ingenious and, in our view, works well in applying the correct braking force in an emergency.

Traction Support Systems

Manufacturers often call these by different trade names, for example some are known as Traction Control. For illustrative purposes we will describe just a couple of the systems. We cannot cover every single type but suffice to say that most operate, in general terms, along the lines described. Those that differ in design terms, even sometimes quite fundamentally, generally provide the same result.

In a strange car, always have a look at the dashboard instruments and visual aids between switching on the ignition and starting up the engine. For example, if an ABS is fitted then there is generally a warning light that comes on when the ignition key is turned. This light goes out soon after you start the engine – once the system has checked itself and it is found to be working correctly. An on/off/status lamp for Traction Control, or similar systems, is likely to be incorporated at close hand to the ABS light(s).

WARNING! Even with a traction support system fitted, you still need a smooth and gentle touch in controlling your car in adverse conditions.

Again, traction support systems work in conjunction with ABS sensors. One of the most common ones monitors the traction of the driven wheels, and then brakes any wheel where wheelspin develops. (Note: if, for example, your car has front-wheel drive, then, this system would operate on the front wheels. However, it is essential to refer to the manufacturer's handbook for an accurate description of the particular type fitted to a car. Indeed, a car may have more than one traction support system.)

In this configuration, if a driven wheel starts to spin, the system intervenes to allow the tyre to regain its grip on the road. This it does by automatically applying the correct amount of braking to that wheel. In effect it slows the spinning wheel until it is revolving at the same speed as the non-spinning wheel of the same pair of [front or rear] wheels. This mates the traction and grip between both tyres concerned and the road surface, in an even manner, so that overall forward traction grip is restored or at least better maintained. The letters ASR (Automatic Skid Reduction) are sometimes used to denote this type of system.

Unfortunately, when fitted to high performance cars, these system(s) can sometimes be overridden by the sheer power of the engine – if you don't 'instinctively' also ease your throttle at the time. Therefore the system is not necessarily foolproof when fitted to very powerful cars and, for this reason, an ESP (Electronic Stability Programme) may be more suitable.

An ESP uses a torque intervention device. When the sensors detect a spinning road wheel, a signal is sent to the engine management system which effectively limits the power of the engine until grip is regained. The system overrides the driver who applies too much throttle, by reducing engine power rather than braking the spinning road wheel as in an ASR system. As a result you cannot fool the ESP, even if you are heavy footed in error. Some vehicles combine an ESP with an ASR and this goes quite some way towards the best of both worlds.

In-Car Safety Features

We all expect and rely on the latest technological safety features to protect us in the event of an accident. Motor manufacturers spend vast amounts on research and development of them, and on stronger, lighter materials, too, so that they can be the first to announce new technology to the market place.

Although seat belts have been fitted in cars for several decades it is still a common (and, mostly, illegal) sight to see them not being used. No matter how good a safety feature may be, if it is not used it cannot do its job! The belief that an accident will never happen on the short journey to the shops, or wherever, is naïve in the extreme as most accidents occur remarkably close to home. Sometimes they are not used out of pure laziness; however, if such drivers had to deal with serious injury accidents, day after day, they would soon see the folly of their ways.

Many cars are now fitted with various types of air bag to cushion your body in the event of an accident. The most popular position is in the centre of the steering wheel in order to protect your chest as driver. However, air bags are now being fitted to cover other parts of the car and protect more occupants. Some air bags are *not suitable for children* and can cause them injury. Find out what the car dealer recommends in this respect before taking children anywhere. Do remember this should you ever borrow or rent another vehicle.

A further development is air bag 'curtains' that are fitted to large areas of the car in order to provide as much protection as possible for the driver and passengers.

Head Restraints

Head restraints are an often underrated and under-utilised piece of safety equipment. Yet, they can reduce significantly the effects of whiplash in an accident. Head restraints can only do their job properly if they are set at the correct height to cushion your head as it moves backwards in a collision. Some cars have head restraints fitted to the rear seats and these should also be adjusted individually. We feel that you as driver should always take responsibility to ensure that everyone in

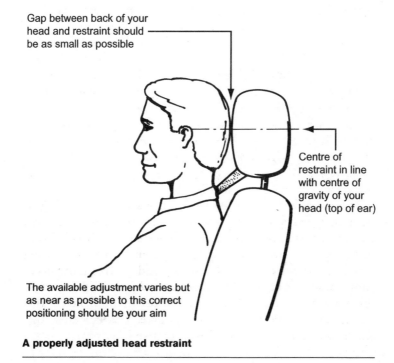

Gap between back of your head and restraint should be as small as possible

Centre of restraint in line with centre of gravity of your head (top of ear)

The available adjustment varies but as near as possible to this correct positioning should be your aim

A properly adjusted head restraint

the car has their seat belt on and their head restraint adjusted to the correct height. Surely that is not asking too much?

Automatic Door Locking

Automatic door locking is a relatively new feature which locks your doors as you drive away. Some drivers/passengers feel the sound of the doors locking is comforting, whilst others feel somewhat claustrophobic. It certainly helps prevent the opportunist thief getting access to your car, for example, at traffic lights but, in an emergency, it does slow down access for a would-be rescuer. We personally would certainly recommend you locking your doors, whether automatically or manually, should you feel vulnerable when travelling at night or in areas where you do not feel safe. However, the choice and responsibility for any consequences – either way – must remain yours.

Limited Slip Differential

The differential fitted between each front or back pair of driven wheels of all cars is there to allow those wheels to travel at different speeds when cornering. As a car goes round a bend, an inner wheel transcribes a tighter bend than an outer wheel, and must therefore rotate more slowly. Without a differential, one or other of the wheels would have to slip on the road surface. The disadvantage of a differential is that, by its very design, it will, in slippery conditions, let one wheel spin during acceleration whilst allowing the other to idle – even though that wheel is gripping the road surface. The net result is that the car hardly accelerates at all.

To overcome this problem on high performance cars and some cross country vehicles, a device is often fitted in the differential to restrain the slipping wheels from doing so. In this way traction is better maintained on both the wheels concerned. On high performance cars the device is a great safety aid. This is because, as you re-accelerate during the course of a bend, and whilst the main weight of the car remains shifted towards your outside wheel(s), there is a tendency to find that wheelspin can be easily induced at your inside wheel(s). (Grip is much reduced at your inside wheel(s) because your vehicle weight is being correspondingly lifted off them.) The limited slip device in the differential immediately counters this tendency for the inside wheels concerned to spin.

Four-wheel-drive vehicles generally have three differentials. One between the front wheels, one between the rear ones and a third located within the drive train that connects the engine to both pairs of wheels. The latter 'central' differential is there to allow the front and rear pairs of wheels to be driven at slightly different speeds, as is required during cornering. However, the combined effect of the three differentials is such that, in very slippery conditions indeed, it is actually possible for only one wheel to rotate whilst the other three idle. Having a limited slip device on the centre differential ensures that at least one wheel of each pair is not idling. On very sophisticated set-ups there would be a limited slip device on all three differentials to ensure all four wheels can best provide traction.

A more basic system on some cross-country vehicles is a differential lock fitted to the central differential. As its name implies it locks the differential rather than limiting the slip. The device is very effective in providing traction for at least one wheel of each pair in super-slippery conditions but, as soon as firm ground is regained, the device must be disconnected to prevent damage to the transmission system.

Some four-wheel-drive vehicles use traction support systems, rather than these differential devices, to maintain traction.

Other Safety Equipment

We tend to take some safety devices too much for granted – for example, your rear view mirrors, one of our greatest safety aids. Whilst your interior mirror probably gets adjusted quite often, your outside mirrors may reflect another story – especially if tricky to adjust from inside your car. So, before you drive away, reject all excuses and make sure you position all your mirrors properly, inside and out.

The seating position and steering angle adjustment are also often drivers' forgotten aids. Set each of them both to match your body contours and so that you can drive your car with maximum efficiency and comfort. Make sure you can reach all your controls without straining and that you are still able to move about behind the steering wheel. Above all, you must be able to see properly and hit your brake pedal hard down. If you cannot do either of these your car will need to be further adapted so that you can.

Very few manufacturers fit fire extinguishers. Yet, if you have ever experienced a car fire, you will know how essential they are. Generally, fire stations are situated in towns because that is where the greatest fire risks are. Therefore, if you have a fire out in the countryside or on a rural motorway, it can take some considerable time for the fire brigade to reach you. We recommend you fit an extinguisher sold as being suitable for car fires.

Chapter 10:

Putting it All Together

It is now time to examine how you fit together all the elements of driving thus far revealed by our detailed analysis. To do so, let's take a journey from what might be your home on the edge of a busy urban area, to a more serene, rural town 15 miles away.

If you haven't given your vehicle a check round pretty recently, you first determine that everything essential is in proper working condition. You take the necessary few minutes to check all the various fluid levels round the engine and including your windscreen washers front and back, and to see to it that your windscreen and other windows, lights, and all your mirrors are really clean. Eyeball your tyres and test that all your exterior lights are fully functional.

If you are borrowing a car you have not driven recently, you do all the same things but also spend a little extra time familiarising yourself with its major controls and switches – and you check up whether or not it has an ABS (Anti-lock Braking System), Traction Control or any other systems about which you might need to know.

Now you get into your car, get comfortable, adjust your mirrors and fasten your seat belt. Ignition 'on' and check your gauges and warning lights. Depress your clutch and start the engine. Then check your gauges and warning lights again. OK? If yes, then you are ready to move off down your driveway.

However, before doing so, you have already started observing and planning your drive, which process will continue to your destination. You have, consciously or subconsciously,

167

asked yourself several, pertinent general questions. 'What is the weather like?' 'What mood am I in?' etc., etc. All these focus on your driving; some, if correctly asked, demand self-honesty you may have to battle hard to produce. This morning, on the one hand, you decide you will need your headlights and heated rear screen on. On the other, you feel you have just lost an argument with a member of your family, and you know you will have to take extra care not to allow any residual strong feelings to affect, still less control, your driving.

So, you now move off towards the road, taking advantage of a good opportunity just to check that your brake pedal remains firm. You check at your gateway for pedestrians and other traffic and, when it is clear, you go, turning left along your road. As soon as you join *any* new road you should routinely check your mirrors, so you do that now.

Your road is fairly straight for half a mile and you are planning to turn left at the traffic lights you will then reach. On the run to the lights you continually scan all around,

You are turning left at these traffic lights

including regular, mirror checks and react accordingly. Already you are forming your Driving Plan for your left turn there. You consider the three essential pre-conditions of all manoeuvres – 'safety, legality and consideration for others'. Your planning includes gathering information, the need for a signal, positioning, adjusting your speed and selecting the correct gear.

There is a lot of traffic all around and so you give an early left indicator and hold to a line well towards the nearside, to indicate your intentions to the drivers already behind. As you do so, you see that the lights are changing to red, so you ease your throttle and start to slow down, checking that the driver immediately behind you has noticed. He, too, is slowing down, so there is no need this time to give a confirmatory flash of your brake lights. Red has appeared and, once you stop, you apply your handbrake, select neutral and take a relaxed view [on life], removing your foot from the brake pedal.

Not too relaxed we would hope! Whilst waiting you re-check your dashboard gauges and continue to look around. In particular, even though, today, you are front marker, you are going to want to know whether anyone may be coming up on your inside on two wheels. You notice from this front position (as you often have before), that you can just see the traffic light facing the crossing traffic. As that light goes amber you select first gear early and make your final checks all around, behind and beside you, that ensure it will be safe for you to go as the light facing you changes to green. Today – after a final look to make certain no crossing driver is still doing so, shooting the red, and no one turning right from ahead is trying to jump the gun – you see no problems so you re-check your nearside and, if clear, pull away and turn left.

There is no other driver to acknowledge and, as you accelerate smartly away, you have time to check your mirrors and reflect on the manoeuvre. What did you notice about it? What *didn't* you notice until surprised to see it in your mirrors? Perhaps you failed to scan sufficiently because your mind was still on that family disagreement!

Forget the argument; concentrate on your driving.

Similarly, how did your turn affect others who were there? Let's assume that today you did well; apart from letting a smidgeon of that earlier cross word intrude whilst you were waiting at the lights.

Shortly the speed limit changes to 40 mph, so you increase your speed a little, still mindful of the high weight of traffic so far. Ahead you can already see a crossroads sign and you know there is a school crossing as well. It is mid-morning, so the children should be in school but you still watch the school entrance carefully and scan into each side of the crossroads.

After a long, straight section you reach the town boundary, and the 40 mph speed limit ends. Although you can see that the road is widening, a road sign warns of a series of bends and the centre line configuration switches to hazard warning mode. Time to practise cornering using 'balanced throttle' perhaps? (See page 142.)

On approaching any bend you must form your Driving Plan. You first run through your mind the three essential pre-conditions. (Have you got those yet?) You then begin to gather your advance information about the layout of the road, particularly the possible severity of each bend, and the length of view you may have into each one; at the same time you are keeping tabs on other traffic to the front and rear, the likelihood of finding pedestrians on the verge and the condition of the road surface.

You also look to see whether, by repositioning your vehicle on the approaches, you can improve your view round the first and subsequent bends, or whether oncoming vehicles, or the chance some may appear, rules this out. The road today has suddenly cleared, and the first bend is open, so you plan to position towards the crown-of-the-road both to maximise your view and to improve your line through this bend to the left. Because of the hazard-warning status of the centre line you nevertheless decide to remain firmly inside it. All this positioning and vision preparation cohabits shortly with beginning deceleration and, perhaps, a need for moderate braking, followed by slipping down to a more appropriate gear. Do you need a signal? No, not at the moment; your brake lights having come on should suffice.

This Driving Plan seems crowded on paper before you even reach the first bend! However, when in progress at the wheel, provided you prioritise your observation suitably, and gauge your speed to match, there is usually plenty of time for more besides. One thing about a series of bends is that you usually need to modify your speed into the first one, downwards a little more, to allow necessary time to flow forward your Driving Plan preparation for the next bend, as you exit the first one, and so on, for each of those to come.

Today, you enter the first bend at the right speed adding a touch of throttle as your car settles nicely into the bend. You exit it, neatly checking your mirrors as you do so. You manage the second bend in an equally controlled manner, and breathe a sigh of relief as you round into the third, both in full control and well inside that hazard-warning line: that saved you a major line correction as an approaching driver cut the corner without having sufficient view round the bend. He certainly hadn't seen you. Well done!

A short straight, now, allows you a few seconds to reflect on your performance through all three bends as a single piece of driving. You feel that your approach speeds were about right and that you are beginning to get the balance about right, but perhaps the original gear change was a bit rushed. You decided to remain in that gear right through the next two bends but reckon, with hindsight, that one gear further down might have suited the final bend rather better. Something on which to work next time.

You also ask yourself 'How did my handling back there affect anyone else on those bends?' 'Not at all' you are pleased to note. However, you remind yourself how wise it is not to cross the centre line unless you have a complete view of the road well ahead and full knowledge about what is behind.

You also consider how you might have applied the 'balanced throttle' technique further to refine well-balanced control but – and it's a big but – without any risk of reaching into that third bend too fast to stop dead if you had to before vision opened up fully into the straight. 'I'll try "balanced throttle" on some easier, single bends first', is what you conclude.

Soon you see a slower-moving vehicle still some way ahead and you start straightaway to plan for passing it, by checking long-range views ahead and your mirrors. As you scan and plan, you build safety, legality and your potential effect on other road users into your thinking – as always – from the outset. This time you find yourself following the slow vehicle into a bend to the left, and so you drop to a lower gear, to be ready should there be an overtaking opportunity as you exit. In addition, as this bend unwinds, you deliberately set up the only chance to look past him up his inside flank. This good driving enables you to see the advance warning of a crossroads with a 'Give Way' sign against you.

You intend to follow this vehicle to the right

As there is now no chance of an overtake, you simply follow him up to the junction at a safe and acceptable distance behind. Your Driving Plan for the pass suspended, you switch your attention at once to the junction. You need to turn right and are already aware of someone behind you. You signal right in good time to check his reaction. He shifts visibly leftward so you conclude that he is not following you round to the right. This is shortly confirmed when he starts to signal left.

When it becomes your turn you have to edge right up to the Give Way line before you can see much. It really is quite a blind junction but, with your window down and no sound of traffic, eventually you are happy that the road is clear and you drive off to the right, checking your mirrors and the new road ahead, as you accelerate away.

Thinking back briefly on the manoeuvre, you are pleased to note that your correct, waiting position at the Give Way line, sufficiently far forward and with your offside smack on line with the centre line, enabled the driver previously behind you to have enough room to make the left turn he wanted, without having to wait for you to clear.

It is not long before you catch up again with the original, slower-moving vehicle and plan, once more, to pass it. Whenever the right moment comes, you are going to need maximum acceleration to make the pass quickly and efficiently, so you drop down a gear in readiness, using the 'sustain' revs technique (see Chapter 8) to effect a seamless change.

Ever mindful of the three essential pre-conditions, you find it necessary, this time – because the slow vehicle has no windows you can see through – to hold back a little, while you ease out gently to gain a view up its offside. Holding back gains more view for less easing out, making this process much safer; and, because you know there has been nothing behind you since that junction, you are able to omit the more usual, over-your-right-shoulder, 'lifesaver' look before you do ease out here. While in the midst of all these preparations you still watch the slow vehicle itself, like a hawk, lest it should suddenly brake or indicate to pull out. You also scan elsewhere within the foreground so as to be sure you don't miss noticing anything else important.

On this occasion, it is only on the third attempt at easing out, that you finally find yourself with just one more car to pass the other way before there will be a 'go' opportunity: you confirm the absence of anyone turning up behind, signal nonetheless, and begin taking up the remaining gap between you and the slow vehicle – timing this carefully so that you can move out and then put your foot down for full bore accelera-tion – exactly on cue after that last car passes.

This way you anticipate that not one shred of time will be lost before you can safely return to your nearside, without cutting in, and remembering to cancel your indicator if it doesn't do so by itself. You complete your pass without inci-dent or stress but reach the conclusion, as you reassess the manoeuvre afterwards, that the slow vehicle driver did not see your signal and was thus unaware you were coming past. Giving a hoot as you began to overhaul him would have alerted him and might have made things safer had something then appeared coming fast the other way at a critical stage. In addition, you felt that his speed was so low that you would have had a better boost of power in second gear rather than in third gear, which you did use. This would have raised your speed differential in the closing stages and allowed you to move back in more rapidly – again an advantage had someone arrived quickly in the other direction. You decide your goal must be to harness these twin aspects of safety, with greater finesse in future.

Shortly after the overtake, you see 30 mph signs in the distance as you approach a village. After checking your mirrors again, your speed drops down and, in turn, the distance ahead that you are scanning can reduce to some degree. In the village your observation is naturally concentrated a little more closely to your vehicle. Your peripheral vision goes on the alert for pedestrians, open gateways, etc., and more frequent mirror checks begin. You constantly strive for your scanning to catch detail: a pedestrian glances round – is he going to step out? Two children are playing around on the pavement – are they going to dart out? A vehicle is nosing out of a side road – is its driver looking at you? A motorcycle appears behind you – is its rider going to overtake?

As you pass out of the village, you are able to consider those two important questions – 'What did I notice about that section of my driving?' and 'How did my car handling affect other road users?' 'That motorcyclist annoyed me by the way it overtook', you accept; though, to be fair, you add: 'I did not move in at all despite there being room.' 'Must try to control such feelings in future', you then decide. 'Had I moved in, he need not have swerved round as he went past.'

On leaving the village the road opens up and traffic is light. Your advanced instructor introduced you to 'fixed-input' steering on your last track day and the next long, straight section of road gives a good opportunity to practise the skill.

You keep your hands at the 'quarter to three' position, where they are already and, with forefinger and thumb making a 'ring' around the steering wheel rim, just above the central crossbar, yet resting on it, you relax and make a point purposely to sense the feedback the steering wheel is giving you. You make the small steering inputs (that are necessary along any straight) without your hands themselves shifting their position on the steering wheel rim at all. At the end of this straight there is a gentle, open bend to the right and you steer accordingly, still with your hands at one with your steering wheel. On the way round, your hands reach as far as 'twenty past ten' but are still gripping the steering wheel at 'quarter to three' on its rim. Unwinding from there, as you exit the bend, brings your hands back again – still in unison with the wheel – i.e. never shifting from their 'quarter to three' hold on the wheel rim itself. Back on the straight, you find that your hands continue to occupy their natural 'quarter to three' position on the steering wheel rim. Thus, your arms alone flex to steer your vehicle and, to unwind that steering, they simply revert whence they came.

The new long straight to which you have returned gives you the opportunity to assess your competence with 'fixed-input' steering. You quickly realise that, although on the straight you were fine, in the bend you were tending to steer too far and then having to compensate. Next time, you will concentrate on getting that steering input right first time in a single, smooth progression, and likewise as you come to back it off again into the straight.

Your journey is coming to an end and, as you enter the quiet rural district to which you are going, your observation, once more, focuses a little closer to your car. You see a parking space near the shops where you are meeting friends, check your mirrors and give an early signal to inform other traffic.

Once parked you take a couple of minutes to reflect on your journey. The thing you remember most was the aggression you felt towards the motorcyclist in that village. Clearly, you *must* still work on your temper. (Was that argument at home still lingering in the background?) Your cornering and overtaking were fairly good, apart, sometimes, from choice of gear. 'Balanced throttle' remains outstanding as something to try on some easy, open, single bends first of all, and 'fixed-input' steering shows promise but needs more practice.

One nagging concern has surfaced now you have switched off your ignition: you recognise that, at no stage of the journey, did you seriously think twice in terms of contingencies, i.e. how you might have revised any one of your Driving Plans instantly had trouble struck. You were not – *and you should have been* – driving so as to maintain a zone of safety permanently available around you, in which to take emergency, evasive action.

As you remove valuables from view and lock your car securely from opportunist thieves and joyriders, you should always – as in the above journey – be able to say, 'I can do better but, at the very least, nothing much was left to chance that I could have done something about.'

Developing and improving all your driving attitudes and skills should be your target throughout your driving career – knowing that perfection, like the end of a rainbow, is far too elusive ever to find.

Chapter 11:

Behind the Wheel

If you take up the expert driving this book explores you should soon habitually be learning ever more about the art of driving safely, smoothly, courteously and considerately. Instead of becoming routine or dull, your driving should blossom with renewed interest and expertise every time you get behind the wheel.

Beyond new skills attained lies the critical element in safe driving – your mental approach. If you ever cease paying attention or you overstretch your ability, you risk accidents. Some research into police road accident involvement is instructive here:

Percentage	Cause
37%	Lack of attention
14%	Loss of control in pursuit
14%	Loss of control on emergency call
7%	Going too fast
7%	Miscellaneous
21%	Lack of care whilst reversing!

Nearly all these demonstrate a poor mental approach at some level, including carelessness and, in particular, driving beyond their personal level or expertise. To be fair to the police, they sometimes have to drive fast but this provides all the more reason to develop their mental control.

The same piece of research also showed that the level of training did not correlate with the likelihood of the police driver having an accident. Officers at all stages of training and experience were having as many accidents as each other. Surprisingly, it was the officers that had no training at all that had slightly less than the others. (One explanation is that they were under less pressure.)

Thus, it was reasonable to say that the skill level and capability of the police drivers did not affect the accident levels. The accidents were caused when those drivers tried to exceed their individual capabilities or were being careless. It was their mental approach and not their skill or capability levels that was the key factor.

The same applies with the general public, where new drivers are more likely to have an accident than more seasoned motorists. This, in our view, is not always, as many believe, because of a lack of skill but, rather, is due to poor mental control.

The mental element of safe driving, then, deserves more recognition than has been accorded it in the past. However, it will be of no avail unless we can all deliver better, more developed attitudes backed by greater knowledge all round.

Attitude development, therefore, must become, for the expert driver, an integral, ongoing part of driving. By using our key, self-assessment questions, 'What did I notice about that section of my driving?' and 'How did it affect other road users?' on a daily basis, you become more self-aware of your state of mind at the wheel, your level of concentration and your attitude in all its myriad facets.

This way you really can change your driving for the better. By identifying your weaknesses through self-assessment you can work on them, turn the tables, and make those areas into new strengths. Whilst on a course you would have an instructor to highlight areas you need to work on but most of us need to manage without such advice the majority of the time. However, provided you continue to be self-aware, you will continue to develop as a driver. If you cease to work at being self-aware, you will regress. A driving course is great if you take home the ability to consolidate and develop. If it becomes history your driving will not be any better.

On the way to becoming an expert driver, improvements in your mental approach should manifest themselves in all sorts of ways:

Thinking and Acting at a New Level

Your ability to act and react should be enhanced. Although you have more information to think about because your improved observation levels mean that you see far more of what is going on around you, your greater awareness also gives you more time. This is because you not only see things earlier but also begin to anticipate what is going to happen from the clues you see. As a potentially dangerous situation develops, you will already be slowing down and taking avoiding action. For example, you will know that a car overtaking towards you is running out of time for returning to his own side possibly before he even knows it himself; whereas less-aware drivers would not recognise the potential danger, perhaps even until it was almost on top of them.

Emotional and Mental Stability

Naturally, all drivers have good days and bad days emotionally. An expert driver, however, becomes more adept at not allowing such other things to cloud his mind while driving. He knows that, if an upset is not supplanted properly by the other priorities of here and now, it will lead to a greater risk of an accident as his mind wanders constantly between his driving and the upset. So, he sharpens his concentration levels by challenging his driving against higher standards than those he might normally accept, thus generating more effective, immediate engagement on the job in hand. In the same way that he would not drive whilst using a mobile telephone, his personal resolve is 'Never drive with other things on your mind'.

Of course, this may not be enough. You cannot always leave

everything outside the car when you sit behind the wheel. Some emotions inevitably follow you into your driving seat. You cannot entirely stop especially painful thoughts flowing into your mind. What you can do is try to minimise their effect as above *and* learn to recognise defeat should they ever temporarily take over – blanking out your concentration on the road. If you are, for whatever reason, ever as deeply upset as that, then you should be aware that it is not a time to drive. Accept this with the strength of mind to stop. It is time, instead, to go for a walk, have a cup of coffee or whatever you need to calm down and stabilise your emotions – even put your car keys away in a secure place for a few days, if that is what it takes to stay safe.

Self-control in all Situations

Many accidents are caused by the driver losing self-control. It is easy to get carried away and try to drive beyond your own or the car's capabilities. How many drivers get themselves into difficulties when they first pass their driving test and think they are the best driver ever? They tear about all over the place trying to defy the laws of physics. If they are lucky, they have a few close scrapes and begin to calm down. Unfortunately, quite a few only learn a salutary lesson by being involved in an accident.

The worst possible scenario is the inexperienced, young driver, showing off to friends or being egged on by them to attempt more than that of which he is capable. It is tempting to drive fast and experience the thrill of it all. It feels good for the ego if your passengers think you can drive like a racing driver. Strangely, some ego tripsters also consider it fun to frighten passengers out of their wits! Unfortunately, these situations can so easily end in tears when the inexperienced and often – but not always – young driver suddenly finds he is driving outside his depth of competence. The accident that almost invariably results, and all its dire consequences, are a hard way to learn self-control.

Even experienced drivers can lose their self-control at times.

Being late for a meeting can lead to trying too hard and exceeding their capabilities. Being delayed by a traffic jam can have the same effect once the traffic clears. Rushing the kids to school can make them do things they wouldn't normally countenance.

As an expert driver you must do better than that! You must demonstrate self-control at all times – constantly aware of your standard of driving and the effect it is having on other people. You must be aware of your limits, and those of your car, and always be driving within them.

Developing Tolerance

A growing trend is a lack of tolerance for one's fellow road users. We even see so-called 'road rage', where one driver cannot accept the actions of another. It makes no difference that the one may have done exactly the same thing himself a short while previously. Unfortunately, this can lead, in a few cases, to an assault and even to injury or death. For someone to die simply because of such a motoring incident is a tragedy and stupidity in the extreme. It is sad that apparently some of us can tolerate so much less from our fellow human beings when we are driving a car than when we are face-to-face.

Lack of forgiveness is very much a fundamental attitudinal trait that can easily be exacerbated by a bad state of mind. An intolerant driver is quite usually always relatively unforgiving of fellow motorists, and it is only the degree of intolerance that varies on a day-to-day basis.

As with many attitudinal disorders, it may take a lot of effort and much time for that person to learn to be more tolerant. If such a person simply trusts his intelligence he will then become hungry to stem his intolerance. This is because he will now understand the value of co-operation and friendliness on which he is presently losing out. This part only he can do. A profound experience, such as a serious accident, sometimes triggers this yearning but all it really needs is for the person concerned to want hard enough to amend his ways. Nothing need then lie between him and success with changing his unforgiving mental approach.

An expert driver will have developed greater tolerance by becoming aware of his attitude to other drivers and by constantly addressing the effect of his driving on other road users. An intolerant driver needs to follow the identical route, knowing only that the journey will be harder and longer but that the reward in terms of personal fulfilment will be that much greater.

Positive Thinking

Part of being an expert driver is being positive in the way you act and control your car. Sound planning brings a positive drive because good observation, underpinned by firm Driving Plans flowing from one manoeuvre into the next, make it so. You will not drift into tricky situations: rather you will find that you know what you intend and are equally able to revise your Plans if things change. Indecision should be a thing of the past because you have made the greater decision that good forward planning supplant it.

Other Driver Behaviour and How to Cope with it

Some drivers are timid and indecisive. Others are aggressive and rude. Thankfully, most are level-headed, and somewhere in between!

When you have to deal with a timid driver there is no point in getting irritated by his lack of decisiveness. Sounding the horn, flashing your lights, or brandishing finger or fist will only make matters worse and could cause the timid driver to do something silly and lose control. An expert driver simply understands that the proper answer is to be patient and let the timid driver sort himself out and go through with his manoeuvre at his own pace. All you can do is give him plenty of room in order to reduce any pressure he might feel from close traffic and to increase your own safety margins lest he finally do something unexpected.

Aggressive drivers are best dealt with by means that are likely to calm them down, rather than inflaming the situation. So retaliatory performances are out. They only make matters worse and result in even more aggression coming your way. An expert driver should have sufficient mental control to ignore the aggression and react positively but politely. In this way the situation can be defused and safety maintained. For example, if someone insists on cutting in front of you as you approach a traffic queue, then you achieve nothing by trying to block him out. All you are likely to receive is abuse and rude signs. Just hold back and let him in with a polite wave if it is appropriate. You cannot change the way people are from your driving seat: you *can* maintain safety levels. Stay calm and stay alive.

Chapter 12:

Motivation

The wonderful thing about people is that we are all delight-fully different. What motivates some of us will be a turn-off for others. Some prefer more carrot and others more stick. How-ever, the best form of motivation – for which expert driving is no exception – is that which comes from within. If you are self-motivated you will work towards your goals without rely-ing much at all on assistance from anyone else. Some drivers are motivated by their profession (e.g. a police driver) and some by order of a court (e.g. a training course as an alternative to punishment). However, with most people it has to come from a simple, self-driven desire to be a better, safer driver.

No matter how motivated you are there will be times when your enthusiasm will wane, only for it to recover in a day or two. This closing chapter seeks to reassure you that you will reach your goal of becoming an expert driver even though the journey there may at times be difficult.

Checking your Progress

Your driving will hopefully by now be different – very different. If you continue to assess your driving and yourself, you will be aware of the progress you are making and be able to judge how to improve still further. Sometimes you can help friends and vice versa, but always remember the latter demands good listening skills, and engaging your brain on their ideas, not yours. Some instructors or mentors can prove hugely beneficial in tuning your driving mindset and skills but your actual progress is largely down to yourself. Acknowledge your achievements when things go right and fight harder when they do not. It will be the continued self-assessment and analysis of your driving that will count in the end. Many drivers already do this. You can too.

One way to assess your progress is to score your overall driving and its constituent parts on a scale of one to ten. Write down the skills and attitudes that you feel are important and, on another sheet of paper placed alongside, enter your scores out of ten. For example, if you choose cornering as an important skill, write it down and put a score next to it that accurately reflects your ability at that time. As you have been working on your cornering skills you may feel you warrant a score of seven. As you have shown impatience recently you may only score yourself at four for that area of your attitude.

Rate yourself every week and see how you have progressed in the areas you have chosen. Remember you are scoring yourself against an ideal rather than a rating improvement. Whilst rating your current performance be careful to hide the previous scores so they do not influence the new ones. You can easily do this by covering them with the list sheet each time. Resist any temptation to score yourself higher than you deserve. The value of this exercise depends on how honest you are with yourself. You will never have to reveal your ratings to anyone else, so you can afford to be totally truthful.

After six weeks or so, review your progress and see whether you wish to change the areas you are assessing. You may have started to develop a new skill and wish to add it to your list. You may feel that other areas have been developed as far as you can for the time being, so give them a rest until the time is right to concentrate on them again. The choice is yours; it is your development and you are responsible for whatever you achieve.

You will come across drivers who appear to have no interest in safety and have a particularly bad attitude towards everything and everybody. By exercising restraint you not only compensate for their appalling attitudes as best you can but should also keep yourself and others safe. Letting others benefit from your expertise is far more satisfying than giving vent to aggression.

Finding the Inspiration to Persevere

Maintaining your expert driving enthusiasm is difficult, at times; make no mistake. Some driving days you will naturally have the motivation, and practising your techniques will be a joy. On others, you will wake up and find it difficult to apply yourself to the task if you take the wheel. Never get desperate or despondent; on the good days enjoy yourself and on the bad at least do whatever you can. Indeed, a bad day can be turned round if you manage a noticeable improvement in something you are working on.

If either of us had to begin the process of reaching out towards expert driving all over again, we certainly would – and with just as much enjoyment. You should find that too. You will not want to go back to your old ways. Every time you get into your car you will want to use it as an opportunity to improve, not simply as a means of transport.

Sometimes your pace may seem slow but, at others, you will leap ahead. Remember you are training your mind as well as your skills. It is easy to monitor your progress when working on a technique; you can observe and feel the improvement. Improving your attitude is more difficult, in the initial stages, both to achieve and to monitor. Attitudinal change, as we noted in Chapter 11, can take considerable time. You will not notice it at first but gradually those who travel with you will begin to make comments on your improvement. Nothing motivates as much as recognition from your peers.

Becoming an expert driver is worth all the hard work. Great fun, greater safety and the immeasurable pleasure of a very personal sense of achievement are your just rewards. You should never stop learning – we all have something to learn about driving, and always will.

We mentioned at the beginning of this book that a perfect

driver has never been born and the perfect drive has never taken place. Nevertheless, you must be positive and aim high. Expert driving is not just a mechanical thing. It demands your innermost spirit of adventure and achievement.

Finally, remember that safety is your prime driving goal. All other goals pale into insignificance against this. Provided you never let safety out of your sight, you will, we hope, one day appreciate that you now qualify as a member of a very select group – expert drivers.

Appendix

VENUES FOR FURTHER TRAINING

Details of your nearest advanced, skid, or off-road training facility can normally be obtained from the following sources:

Local Driving Instructor/School

Your local driving instructor/school should have an interest in further training and be able to direct you to the nearest facility.

Institute of Advanced Motorists (IAM)

The IAM will be able to give you guidance on seeking further training and details of your local branch office can be obtained from: Head Office, IAM House, 510 Chiswick High Road, London, W4 5RG. Telephone 020 8996 9600.

Motoring Organisations

The AA and RAC have departments that deal with further training and details of these can be obtained by referring to their entries or advertisements in your local telephone directory.

Police Driving Schools

Police driving schools concentrate on training their own staff but many also provide some training for the public. Furthermore, they should be aware of other training facilities in their area. Contact your local constabulary headquarters and ask to be put through to their driving school. Some forces share facilities so you may be referred on.

Driving Standards Agency (DSA)

The DSA may be able to direct you to local facilities and they can be contacted at Stanley House, 56 Talbot Street, Nottingham, NG1 5GU or by telephone: 0115 901 2500.

Motoring Magazines

Appropriate magazines will carry advertising/give details about circuit driving and track-driving clubs.

SKID CAR is a Swedish developed system which can be used on many types of vehicle to simulate skidding conditions. The equipment is in training use with the police, the armed forces and at such places as racing circuits. For location details visit their website at www.skidcar.co.uk

Royal Society for the Prevention of Accidents (RoSPA)

RoSPA's purpose is to enhance the quality of life by exercising a powerful influence for accident prevention. The RoSPA Advanced Drivers' Association offers training and testing at the highest level. Telephone: 0121 248 2000.

Index

More Driving Sense

VERY ADVANCED DRIVING

Author Tom Topper's unique, practical, "in situ" insights have shaped higher road driving skills for over three decades.

Now in its 7th edition his book debunks the myth that speed kills, by demonstrating what are the actual causes; invites controversy by showing how the 70 mph, national speed limit is a prime cause of bunching and M-way madness; and contributes for debate powerful, fresh ideas on how the police could be empowered with a new, educational role – one for which they are uniquely suited and through which they could largely jettison the negative image too many of them have rapaciously acquired.

Above all, the lively thrust of Topper's pen subtly re-shapes your motoring psyche. You won't put this book down until you become a VERY ADVANCED [Driving] thinker, qualified to dip again among its challenging pages, and again, and again.

Very Advanced Driving is also published in Right Way.